Life with a Partner or Spouse with Asperger Syndrome:

Going over the Edge?

Practical Steps to Saving You and Your Relationship

Life with a Partner or Spouse with Asperger Syndrome:

Going over the Edge?

Practical Steps to Saving You and Your Relationship

By Kathy J. Marshack, Ph.D.

Foreword by Stephen Shore, Ed.D.

APC

Autism Asperger Publishing Co.
P.O. Box 23173
Shawnee Mission, Kansas 66283-0173
www.asperger.net

P.O. Box 23173
Shawnee Mission, Kansas 66283-0173
www.asperger.net • 913.897.1004

Publisher's Cataloging-in-Publication

Marshack, Kathy, 1949-

Life with a partner or spouse with Asperger syndrome : going over the edge: practical steps to saving you and your relationship / by Kathy J. Marshack. -- 1st ed. -- Shawnee Mission, Kan. : Autism Asperger Pub. Co., c2009.

p. ; cm.

ISBN: 978-1-934575-47-5
LCCN: 2009923446
Includes bibliographical references.

1. Asperger's syndrome--Patients--Family relationships. 2. People with mental disabilities--Marriage. 3. Interpersonal communication. I. Title. II. Title: Going over the edge.

RC553.A88 M37 2009
616.85/8832--dc22 0903

Cover Illustration: Anonymous artist

Cover Background: ©mittymatty istock photo

This book is designed in Blaze and Minion.

Printed in the United States of America.

Dedication

While there are so many loved ones, clients, friends, colleagues and supporters without whom this book would never have been completed, there is one man who sparked me to start writing. And starting is the hardest thing to do. Gary Blackton, my longtime friend and advisor, may never know how much his love and inspiration has meant to me, since he has now passed on. I hope he knows. When Gary looked me in the eye one day and told me that this story had to be told, I knew I would be the one to do it.

Table of Contents

Foreword

If you are reading this book, you may have picked it up because you have been asking yourself, "Is it me or is it my spouse?" Dr. Marshack yanks you in with vivid storytelling about people married to a partner with Asperger Syndrome. In an Expressionist manner, with raw and exposed examples cutting to the emotional core of the human condition, we see how difficulties in "mixed marriages" where one member of the couple is on the autism spectrum can lead the non-spectrum spouse (as well as the one with Asperger Syndrome) to the very edge of violence, divorce, and questioning of his or her sanity.

However, marriage to a person with Asperger Syndrome does not have to be this way, as the reader finds out from the many practical tips and *Lessons Learned* in the following pages. The good news is that this book describes only some spectrum-non-spectrum marriages. There are many successful "mixed" marriages and long-term relationships in which one partner is on the autism spectrum and the other is not.

What explains the difference in marital success met by the latter couples versus what can be the destruction of a spouse or partner's emotional being, as described in the book you are about to read? The answers lie in the *Lessons Learned* at the end of each chapter and the practical solutions to the challenges laid before couples when Asperger Syndrome is thrown into the relationship mix.

Almost any reader who is married will see pieces of his or her relationship challenges described in the following pages. Just as accentuated strengths combined with significant challenges are characteristic of children with autism, the same dynamic of extremes plays out in marriages and long-term relationships where Asperger Syndrome is present. Part of this challenge arises from the two different "operating systems" of spectrum and non-spectrum running in one relationship, which tends to confound communication in particular. Whereas the non-spectrum spouse may be tuned into the nonverbal communication of social interaction at a party, for example, the Aspie partner may be desperately trying to avoid sensory overload by focusing on the number of tiles in the ceiling instead of the conversation going on around him. Take it from one who knows – having resorted to that very same thing on numerous occasions.

In our marriage my wife and I work together on these challenges. Seeing my discomfort, she may recommend that I take a break. Additionally, I have learned to reference her body language to give me gigabytes of information, ranging from whether I am breaking a social rule to the fact we are leaving in about five minutes. A lack of understanding on her part might result in damaging battles between the two of us centered on my lack of proper comportment at the social event.

The *Lesson Learned* about anger being a healthy signal is a very important one. For a long time, as for many on the autism spectrum, anger was a very difficult and unpredictable emotion for me that, when coming from my wife or others close to me, could feel like the end of the world. However, over time, I have realized that it is important for my wife to talk about her anger, thereby releasing the emotion rather than allowing it to build up to a Mt. Vesuvius-worthy explosion, as described in this book. At the same time, my wife understands my need for taking "time-outs" when the conversation becomes too heated for me.

Another *Lesson Learned* focuses on communication. It is commonly acknowledged that a certain amount of mind reading occurs between partners, giving rise to the refrain "I should not have to tell you what I am angry about." For a partner on the spectrum, this can lead to utter confusion. My wife and I figured out pretty early in our relationship the importance of communication in a marriage that is mixed on a number of vectors, including race and nationality – she immigrated from the People's Republic of China to the United States and I am a fourth-generation American. This, combined with my being on the autism spectrum and she being non-spectrum, makes it imperative that we verbalize our feelings a lot more than most other couples. Knowledge is power. And the knowledge that we have vastly differing backgrounds requiring more verbalization makes our marriage stronger. In some ways, the Asperger Syndrome helps glue our marriage together.

The *Lesson Learned* related to acceptance is another dab of glue holding our marriage together. My wife understands that I may not socialize with her friends on the same level as she does when we go to their homes for a visit. My preferences for playing with their cats, going online, or even departing with a promise to pick her up some hours later may baffle her. I often am unable to draw sense out of why she can talk endlessly about a problem she is having with one of her music students when I just want to make a suggestion and then get on with my activities. However, I trust that this is something she needs to do and leave it at that. *We accept each other as we are* and realize that no matter how hard we try, it is not possible, and indeed not really desirable, to change the other person.

Another important thing to realize is that practically everything described in this book happens in many marriages where there is no Asperger Syndrome present. Also, it only happens in *some* spectrum-non-spectrum marriages and relationships – by no means all.

Yet, as Dr. Marshack so clearly depicts, when there is a lack of understanding, things can get bad. However, great benefits from the *Lessons Learned* of focusing on the [often unique] qualities in an Asperger's loved one can bring great rewards. For example, my deep passion for airplanes and travel has taught me how to secure the best seats on a plane and how to swiftly navigate through airports – a skill that came in very handy when my wife and I traveled 24 hours to get from Boston to Beijing one summer. On the other hand, my wife has great skill in planning our travel itinerary once we get to our destination. And I am happy to leave that job to her.

Loyalty is a fundamental value in a marriage. People with Asperger Syndrome tend to be very loyal – even if they don't express it in words. I heard of a wife who remarked to a counselor once that she was not sure that her husband, who was on the autism spectrum, loved her any more. After all, he had not uttered the three magic words often repeated between significant others – "I love you." Upon questioning by the counselor, the husband responded that he told his wife that he loved her several years ago and that it had not changed. So why should he repeat himself? Now that she knew the reason why, his wife felt much better. Additionally, now that the husband realized that these three words were important to his wife, he began to say them to her once in a while. Change is possible if mutually agreed upon.

This book may be difficult and challenging to read at times, as its hard-hitting examples and arguments force readers to take stock of their own relationships and relate to feelings they may have or have had about their spouses and significant others. However, the knowledge gained from the examples and practical tips throughout the book will promote a more solid and satisfying union between two people. Ultimately, if you are in a successful relationship, many of the stories and ideas expressed here may not apply to you. For better or for worse, no two relationships are the same.

Stephen M. Shore, Ed.D., assistant professor of education, Adelphi University; internationally known author, consultant, and presenter on issues related to the autism spectrum; member, Board of Directors, the Asperger's Association of New England and the Autism Society of America

INTRODUCTION

Tough Relationships

Asperger Syndrome

I was sitting one day with Zack, a very bright young man with Asperger Syndrome, often referred to as high-functioning autism. At eighteen he was in my office seeking therapy by his parents' request, in hopes that I could help him reduce his anxieties and develop some independence. He was a very likable young man, but it was clear that Zack had a lot of fears about putting himself out there. He talked about attending college but, unlike most teenagers who dream about leaving home when they get disillusioned with their parents, he didn't want to leave his parents' home. He talked about getting a job but made no effort to do so all summer long. He talked about getting together with friends for socializing, but I soon learned that his friends were really family friends who came over to visit his parents – not kids his own age. He talked about spending time with his older brother, but in reality that mainly involved his older brother helping out his parents by driving Zack to his appointments. Otherwise, Garrett was seldom home because he had a job, a girlfriend and was off to college in the fall.

It was as if Zack knew that he should be doing more with his life. He could even invent a bit of an independent existence – at least in his mind – but taking action to make it happen was beyond him. Zack is fond of computers, computer games and the Internet, and these are the sum total of his existence.

On this particular day I gently confronted Zack with his lack of follow-through. I didn't want him to feel criticized – again – but I did want to break through his defenses and begin a plan of action. In an attempt to relate to his favorite interest, I suggested that life is like an interactive computer game. It requires taking a few risks and trusting that not all risks turn out badly. Like an interactive computer game, the fun is in the changing nature of the game as the player maneuvers through the game and learns the rules. Zack balked.

"I don't like risk. I don't like to do things that I haven't done before. Gaming is not the same," he said in a wary tone.

"But Zack, you know that you can't learn anything new if you don't try. Sometimes you take a risk and you fail. At other times you take a risk and you win. But even if you fail, you can try taking another approach. Failure is just feedback. Each failure lets you know what doesn't work and opens up other options that might work. Did you know that other people feel nervous about risks, too?"

Zack looked at me with interest. He didn't know that other people worry. I was encouraged.

"Well, I don't like to worry. I like to have a plan." Again the wary tone with an edge to it.

Not one to give up easily, I tried again. "Yes, that's understandable. Most people have a plan when they take on something new. They plan the best they can for something they have never done before. They even have backup plans."

Zack was definitely interested now, as if it had never occurred to him that other people might have fears about new things just like he does. And it had never occurred to him that other people plan for success.

Zack thought long and hard. Then he drew in a big breath and explained, "I know you are trying to help me, but the problem for me is that it feels too scary to try something new when I don't know how it will turn out – no matter how much I plan. The risk just seems too big.

With a computer game, it doesn't hurt so much if you fail. And there is no one there to laugh at you."

This last comment really made me feel Zack's pain. Having Asperger's is like that. It's not just the failures that mount up because relating to others is so darned difficult, it is the associated ridicule and rejection that create the pain that forces so many Aspies into isolation.

Even though I was having trouble getting Zack past his fears, at least I could let him know that he was not alone. I wanted him to know that I understand his fears and that I have helped others conquer theirs. "Zack, take a look at this drawing by a young woman who has Asperger Syndrome just like you." I showed Zack a drawing of a young girl pole vaulting off a cliff with nothing underneath her or on the opposite side to jump to – the very same picture that is on the cover of this book.

In his quiet way, Zack looked at the drawing, and with a flat tone he said, "Yes, that is exactly it. When I jump, I don't know if there will be rocks or water at the bottom."

Defining Asperger Syndrome is not easy, since it is a compilation of many traits that come together in an often-confusing picture of disability that can hold people back from life indefinitely. Taking every word literally, mind blindness (or not knowing how others think) and a consequent lack of empathy are hallmarks of Asperger Syndrome. But so too are many other traits, depending upon how much of the disorder a person has.

For example, many people with Asperger Syndrome have extreme sensory awareness. The pulsing of fluorescent lights or the pungent fragrance of cologne can be so distracting that they become ill. While the rest of us are not as sensitive and are better able to screen out unwanted stimuli – or even enjoy them – those with Asperger Syndrome are so unnerved by the experience that they can become ill. At the very least, this extreme sensitivity is one reason why they hide away from relationships and the cacophony of society.

At the very worst, Aspies can become controlling of their environments and demanding of others to comply with their sensitivity needs. Seen from this point of view, it is understandable why Aspies (individuals with Asperger Syndrome) develop rigid thinking and behavior. It is a form of protection for them, but it often drives away neurotypicals (NTs).

In the scenario with Zack, you can see how literal he is. You can see that he is plagued by his anxieties. He has found a comfortable spot for himself in his room playing computer games – and away from people. Zack also has his share of sensory sensitivities. He hates clothing that scratches and prefers loose-fitting garments – and no seams in his socks to irritate his skin. He prefers to wear the same clothes all of the time since he is familiar with their fit and comfort, and therefore doesn't have to be afraid of new clothing that might not work for him.

Zack has loving parents and is not as frightened as many young adults with Asperger's, but he is starting to get worried that he will be out in the world soon without the protection his parents currently provide.

Zack's mind blindness and inability to empathize with others is revealing. Even when I tell him that another person with Asperger's shares his fears, he can only relate to the young woman's drawing . . . not to her. If Zack cannot fathom where other people are coming from, no wonder he is anxious about taking risks in the interpersonal world of college, work and dating.

Asperger Syndrome is a form of autism that has captured the attention of the media lately because of the unexplainable increase in diagnoses among school-age children. For example, Steve Silberman wrote a piece for *Wired* magazine in December 2001 entitled "The Geek Syndrome" where he speculated on the phenomenal increase of children with Asperger Syndrome living in Silicon Valley with their "geeky" parents. A few months later *Time* magazine ran an article in its May 6, 2002, issue by J. Madeleine Nash entitled "The Secrets of Autism." Nash asked, "The number of children diagnosed with autism and Asperger's in the United States is exploding. Why?"

Over the next few years every major newspaper and magazine in the United States published on the subject, and television and radio have run specials. However, while there has been an anecdote here or there on the subject of adults with Asperger Syndrome, the overwhelming emphasis has been on children and schooling. In fact, so little is written on the subject of adults and adult relationships that Suzanne Leigh of *USA Today* interviewed me for an article entitled, "A long shadow is lifted on Asperger's in adults" published July 23, 2007 . . . before the publication of *Life with a Partner or Spouse with Asperger Syndrome: Going over the Edge?* . . . because she could find few experts on the subject who have published in the United States.

Clearly, the interest is growing, but the answers are scarce. So the questions remain. What happens when children with Asperger Syndrome grow up? How do they function in the world of relationships when they lack the empathy to connect . . . to truly understand and appreciate the thoughts and feelings of others . . . as different than their own? How do they move past the anxieties that often bury them? How do they learn to take risks when they have the comfort and safety of the computer to occupy their days? In fact, how do they learn about their connection to others and their place in the world without interacting with others?

In this book I hope to steer the focus to the complex world of adult interpersonal relationships. While someone with Asperger Syndrome can be a terrific computer programmer, be successful at raising cattle, or whatever he chooses to do for a living, he also has to live in the world of people. Many with Asperger Syndrome are extremely lonely due to a lack of interpersonal awareness and skill. And these problems lead to severe relationship disorders. Other books on relationship enhancement do not come close to addressing the problems that NTs have with their Asperger loved ones. By reading this book you will learn more about how NTs and Aspies handle and successfully resolve many of their unique relationship problems.

Is This My Story?

When I developed the idea for this book two years ago and crafted the first chapter, many asked if the story of Helen in the following pages is really about me. People tell me the stories are so real and compelling that they could only have been written by someone who has lived this life. My answer is that I am not Helen, but I can relate to her in a big way. Through Helen I came to understand better my own intimate connection with Asperger Syndrome. I cleared up, and I am still clearing up, many misconceptions I have had about the syndrome and about myself. Helen helped with that, even though she does not know it.

Helen is not one person. Neither is Jeri, Emil, Jasmine, Grant, Jason, Mandy and Norman . . . or Zack. They are real people, to be sure, but are disguised to protect their identities and their privacy. On occasion I have taken the liberty of combining lives and altering facts so that the identities are even more protected. I never want to bring distress to these wonderful people who have shared their triumphs and disasters with me. I owe them the courtesy of keeping their lives private. But if you recognize yourself in these pages, it is because, like me, you are living with a loved one who has Asperger Syndrome or you have Asperger's yourself. The similarities that people notice are uncanny, and that is because the NTs and the Aspies among us have a lot in common.

I do share some of my own story in these pages, however. I have family members with Asperger Syndrome, but at their request I am not acknowledging who they are. Since my mother, Irene, has passed on, I do reveal her story. I hope she is proud of how much she has helped me with this book. Besides, what psychologist is worth her salt if she doesn't come to terms with her mother issues? I gladly share this part of the journey, since this book is not just about learning to live with those loved ones who have Asperger Syndrome. Writing this book has also been a journey of personal and spiritual discovery for me.

So in answer to the question, "Is this my story?" I would have to proudly say, "Yes." I hope you too will see yourself in these stories and learn to open up to new ways of conceiving of a relationship with your loved ones.

Hot Debate

Before I published this book, it was hotly debated in the Asperger community with regard to its "political correctness." While some of us work on methods to help Aspies develop more social skills, healthier coping mechanisms and relief from anxiety and depression, others propose that Asperger Syndrome is not a developmental disorder, but merely a different way of being. They propose tolerance for "neurodiversity" and suggest that if left alone Aspies would be free to live life according to the beat of their own drums.

Frankly, I don't see the conflict. Through the stories in this book, I hope you will come to understand better the inner workings of the Asperger mind so that you can love and respect your family member even more and so that you can free yourself to do what is in your best interest. The goal is not for you to learn to change anyone, but to change yourself by coming to a new understanding of yourself and the other in your relationship.

The bottom line is this. NT-Aspie relationships can be tough, and that is no one's fault. First and foremost, it is important to understand that there is no blame. Asperger Syndrome is not a disease. It is a type of brain organization that one is born with, just as those described as NTs have a certain brain organization. Although all of us are unique and none of us have the same set of fingerprints, there are patterns among NTs that are different than the patterns among Aspies. And these differences in brain organization and behavior patterns can create serious interpersonal problems for the NTs and Aspies involved. Often the relationships are so strained that the conflicts escalate to damaging proportions, involving divorce, child abuse, domestic violence, depression and a host of other problems. I think it makes sense to explore these relationships and make an effort to teach others how to do better. That is my attempt in this book and in my practice as a therapist.

Because I am NT, the obvious slant in this book is toward the NT point of view. I have tried to be balanced in my presentation and to show the strengths of Aspies and NTs as well as their limitations. But to be honest, none of us – even psychologists – can hide our innate organization and personal perspective. I have written this book primarily to help NTs learn how to grow up and away from dysfunctional behavior and dysfunctional relationships. But my hope is that there will be Aspie partners, spouses, siblings, parents and children who keep an open mind while reading this book. If we can bring these two worlds a bit closer, that could make a lot of difference in the happiness of many people.

One of my clients, an engineer and an Aspie, had this to say about his marital problems. "It's like my wife and I have different operating systems for our brains." I liked the computer metaphor and asked what he thought the solution would be. He answered, "Well, you can't run each other's software on your brain, so you have to build an interface protocol." I am not very technically savvy, but I like the metaphor. I hope this book will help build an "interface protocol" between the NTs and Aspies in your life.

Layout of the Book

The point of this book is to give you a look into the lives of a handful of people who live with a loved one with Asperger Syndrome. Stories are an ancient method of teaching, and they work as well today as they did during prehistoric times. If by reading these stories you learn more about your own situation and you gain hope, then my goal has been accomplished.

In addition to the stories, I end each chapter with a short section on "Lessons Learned" where I summarize my thoughts on Helen's life (and the lives of the other participants). I will give you a new way to look at these situations and some tips on how to handle similar situations better in your own lives.

Is This Your Story?

Now begins the journey. Take heart and plunge in. You have picked up this book because you want to know more and be more. The question is how to take back your life and still be there for your loved ones. If you are just waking up to Asperger Syndrome and the effect it has had upon you, you may not fully understand what I mean by "taking back your life." But you can feel what I mean. Living in ignorance of the problem and blaming yourself or the other person for a failed relationship is like being sucked into a black hole of nothingness. There is no love in this black hole.

Human beings need each other. We were made for each other. We even have neurons in our brains that respond only to the tiniest of nonverbal human interaction. What this means is that we come to know ourselves in relation to others, especially those we love. Because those with Asperger Syndrome are wired differently in some ways than neurotypicals, there can be a profound disruption in this process of knowing ourselves when NTs and Aspies are in a relationship with each other. And over time NTs can give up knowing who they are because of this lack of feedback and empathy from an Aspie loved one. Some call it depression, but to me it is a loss of a sense of self.

One Aspie husband was aware of this disconnect when his wife asked for a divorce. He wrote her a touching email in which he described his wife's quest for meaning, "You have dreams and want to talk about them. I don't have dreams. I don't know why I don't have dreams."

Through this book you will learn how to take back your life, reinvent yourself and find love again for yourself. Only then can you really be there for your loved ones in return. To look into another's eyes and see the Soul that resides there and to know that another Soul is looking back at you . . . and both are loving each other . . . this is what I mean by taking back your life. I hope that you will have some of that experience in reading this book . . . that there is another who understands and appreciates you.

Now it is time to rewrite your story, to begin the process of taking back your life in relation to your Asperger loved one. It begins with taking a fearless inventory of yourself. After that the sky's the limit.

CHAPTER ONE

Patience Is Not Enough

The story of Helen and Grant begins in this chapter, but it is by no means the beginning of Helen's story. It is only after years of living with an undiagnosed Asperger mate that Helen finally comes to realize that patience is not enough. In this chapter you will learn that you are not alone if you also live with this type of family configuration. For your recovery, it is important to know that you are not alone.

Mind Blindness and Safety

Patience is a virtue, I've been told, but dealing with the mind blindness of an Asperger mate requires more than patience. Mind blindness is the phenomenon whereby Aspies have no idea of what is going on in the mind or life of another person. They cannot put themselves in the other's shoes and anticipate the next step in the conversation or the relationship.

Faced with this, coupled with the Aspie's rigid thinking and anxiety about anything out of the ordinary, many neurotypical (NT) spouses find it necessary to look for methods of coping, even though it is not always productive. NTs make excuses for their spouse's social inadequacies, carry more and more of the load for the relationship or begin to lose their sense of self in the oppression of their Aspie partner's one-sided thinking. Some NT spouses even begin to fear for their personal safety, not so much because of physical violence, but because their partner seems clueless about the safety needs of family members, including children, parents and themselves.

It Must Be in the Details

After a month, I now know enough about Helen to realize that she needs to tell me her stories at length, so I don't interrupt her any more. I let her talk. The content of her life experiences is not as important to Helen as the littlest detail. There is something in the details that holds a key for her. Learning about her through her stories is like reading a mystery novel. Layer after layer of nuance, and thread after thread of subplot, are woven together and lead the listener deeper into Helen's world of loneliness and despair.

In spite of an ostensibly successful career and marriage, Helen sought me out for psychotherapy because she feels empty and disconnected from life. Perhaps a mid-life crisis? She is forty-something, with shoulder-length blond hair and watery gray-blue eyes. She appreciates her tall stature and slender body, dressing in stylish professional attire. Helen is attractive. When she walks into the room, she is noticed. She has a powerful presence, so at least on the surface, it is a mystery that she feels so depressed and unfulfilled.

Others describe Helen as an assertive, articulate and talented professional, and there is no doubt she is a caring and devoted wife and mother. But as Helen weaves her stories of life with her husband and children, there is something she is trying to tell me but can't quite put her finger on. She often refers to it as "the sliver in my mind," as if releasing the sliver will free her of the confusion and suffering she feels.

I recognize that Helen's home life is a bit odd. Her husband, Grant, seems eccentric and immature, but I can't quite identify the problem either. Like Helen, I am worrying a sliver in my own mind. I want to help her, but so far I don't know how, except to listen. I want to understand what stands in the way of a meaningful life for Helen.

CHAPTER ONE

Lying on the Floor

Helen tells me a story.

The room was pitch black, so I knew it was still the middle of the night. I could hear the pulse in my ears and feel the clammy, tingly feeling of the blood rushing into my neck, chest and fingers. I don't know how long I lay unconscious on the bedroom floor, but it could not have been long since my pajamas were still warm with urine from when I lost control of my bladder. I must have fainted when I tried to make that last move to reach the hallway to get to the bathroom.

I lay quietly for a moment, as the consciousness of what had happened started to spread through me. It was another of those many moments that make no sense in my life.

I had awakened in the night with that familiar sensation that I needed to urinate. Grant was sound asleep next to me. I rolled over on my side to get out of bed when I felt an intense bolt of pain rip through my lower back. I moaned and fell back into bed. My husband did not stir.

Wide awake now and breathless, I tried again to get out of bed but did it gingerly because I recognized what I was feeling. I had a pinched nerve in my lower back (it stems from an old injury and occasionally flares up unexpectedly). It would be a long trip to the bathroom.

Inch by painful inch, I moved my half-bent body to the edge of the bed and fell to the floor, gasping for breath as the pain grabbed me by surprise. I was able to hang onto the edge of the bed and creep along the side, but could not stand up. Each time I tried to get up, the pain became so intense that I almost fainted. Periodically, I would stop and take a breather, which would cause more pain. Holding my breath seemed the only way to get to the bathroom. In the meantime, my husband slept on.

Maneuvering around the corner of the bed was another harrowing experience. I took a risk and decided to turn the corner, even though this required some sophisticated movements. I tried to stand and turn at the same time, but I lost consciousness for a moment. Fortunately, I came to in time to grab the footboard and keep from falling. I screamed in pain. Not one sound came from my slumbering husband.

I was gaining some confidence as I inched along the foot of the bed toward the doorway leading to the hall and the bathroom. I was at a crossroads . . . to stand or to crawl the rest of the way since there was no more bed to hang onto. I felt an odd sense of accomplishment that I had made it this far and had not disturbed my husband's sleep. Feeling brave, I stood up, but this time I did not feel the pain or the impact of hitting the floor. A loss of consciousness spared me this suffering, but not the emotional abuse that was to follow.

I felt the warmth of my wet pajamas so I knew I was alive, but I was humbled. I knew I could not get any farther without help. I called to my sleeping husband, but before I could finish saying his name I felt the pain again. Even that little activity pulled the muscles that squeezed the vertebrae. So I tried another tactic. I lowered my voice and spoke from the back of my throat, hoping that he would hear me, wake up and help me. "Grant." There was no response, so I tried again, "Grant, I need help."

This time he did hear me. What a relief! But he responded in his characteristic way that makes no sense at times like this. "What do you want?" he asked.

I have lived with this man for two decades and have become accustomed to his unfeeling style, so I did not skip a beat in responding. He always needs my help in understanding even very simple things. Still speaking slowly so as not to create pain, I said, "Grant, I need your help. I cannot get up. I want you to get up out of bed and come help me stand up so that I can get to the bathroom."

"Now?!" he asked, with incredulity.

"Yes, Grant. I need you to get up and help me. I cannot move. I am in great pain. I fell to the floor because I have a pinched nerve in my back. You must help me get up."

"Oh," he said. "I was wondering what you were doing on the floor."

Grant had been awake the entire time Helen was making her painful journey around the bed and across their bedroom. He observed her with the detached perspective of the man with Asperger Syndrome (AS), unable to "connect the dots," so to speak. He was not in pain, so he could not relate to Helen's pain. It was night and time for sleeping, so he focused on that, failing to understand how to transition to the new situation his wife's odd behavior posed.

Even when he got out of bed to help Helen, she had to instruct him how to lift her to avoid the pain. She had to ask him to get her clean pajamas. She had to ask him to wait for her in the bathroom. She had to ask him to get towels to clean the carpet. She had to ask him to help her back to bed. Even the next morning, she had to remind him that she needed help and ask him to call the chiropractor for an emergency visit. He could not problem solve any of this. Instead of being concerned for Helen's health and well-being, he worried about being late for work when she asked him to drive her to her appointment.

Yes, the details reveal the nature of Helen's life with an Asperger's husband, but how do I help her? Asperger Syndrome is a lifelong condition. Is there another way?

Let Me Guide You Through the Looking Glass

If you live with an Asperger's husband or another family member, I'm sure Helen's story does not seem unusual, even if the details are different. It is part of your everyday life. If you have these experiences but are not sure if your spouse has Asperger Syndrome, you may be startled by the uncanny similarity of your life and Helen's. Some of the facts may change from story to story, couple to couple and family to family, but what is constant are the symptoms of Asperger Syndrome that create chaos, fatigue, insanity – and sometimes heartbreak – in your life.

In this book I will share stories from my life too, because I also have family members with AS. Although some psychologists know a little about AS in children, they know very little about what happens when these children grow up and marry. They don't know the often mind-numbing story that is hidden in the details. Instead of a clinical overview of the disorder, I write stories from the heart, the heart of a woman who lived through a lifetime of extreme pain and loneliness. I know too well how Helen feels.

The loneliness is perhaps the greatest heartache I lived with. It is hard enough to live with someone who is emotionally unavailable, the problem is compounded by having no other person in your life who understands or believes you when you tell them what you are going through. I want those of you who are living this life to know that there is at least one other person who knows. And I want to help you get the life you deserve. Writing this book is doing that for me because it is something I have a passion for and have wanted to do for a long time.

You may not relate to all of my stories or Helen's. Not everyone with AS is the same. Personality and environmental influences affect how we mature. And because AS is a developmental disorder, and a constellation of many traits, not everybody who has Asperger's face the same challenges. For example, Helen's husband is clumsy, has night blindness, can't recognize faces easily, has a volatile temper, is obsessive about work and is addicted to watching television. Another may be artistic, shy, slovenly, anxious, fearful of confrontation and disorganized. Most with AS have several sensory sensitivities, overreacting to loud sounds, intense lighting, strong fragrances or scratchy fabrics. Still others may be hyposensitive and not even notice the strong odors emanating from their unkempt room, or the chill that has crept up after sunset while they sat outside engrossed in a book. But what all those with Asperger's seem to have in common is the effect they have on their loved ones. Because they are not able to empathize, they often leave us feeling alone or crazy, and the relationship often evolves into that of a caretaker to a disabled person.

Through these stories of real people and real lives, I hope you will learn about AS and how to cope with it. You, the caretaker of a partner with AS, will have to do most of the work in the relationship. However, the more you learn about the syndrome, the easier it will become to live your life and disconnect from blame and guilt and the crazy adaptations you have made in order to live with these people.

Looking at the story in this chapter, do you see the craziness? Why didn't Helen ask for help right away when she felt the first bolt of pain?

Why did she assume her husband was asleep, after years of living with this man and knowing better at another level? Why was she proud of taking care of herself? Why did she have to explain the obvious to a grown man? Where is the caring for the caretaker? I will answer these questions and go beyond the usual textbooks on AS, which tend to focus mostly on diagnosis and providing services to the child with AS, and offer little guidance or hope for the adult relationship.

Living with an Asperger's mate is like traveling through the Looking Glass in Lewis Carroll's classical tale. You think you have traveled into another dimension, and like Alice you have no reference points for relating to the situation. I want to give you those reference points, so that you can navigate this world. And I want you to go beyond mere survival in the Asperger's Dimension. Once you know the territory, you can choose to stay or leave . . . at will. That is important. That is freedom!

At this point in the story and your personal self-discovery, you may not know what I mean by reference points or freedom. If you are living with an Asperger's mate, child or parent, you may feel trapped. At times, you might even feel as if you are in prison, or ready to go over the edge. Learn how to gain the freedom to take back your life. Patience is not enough. You must be brave, and you must take action if you are to get out of the war zone and create the life you deserve.

Lessons Learned

1. Trust your intuition. If the situation seems crazy, maybe it is.
2. Seek professional help from someone who knows about the interpersonal dynamics of Asperger Syndrome – not just the diagnosis, but what it is like to live with an Aspie.
3. Read this book over and over again and take it with you wherever you go, so that you will know that you are not alone.
4. Caretaking can be an expression of love, but if the result is a loss of your sense of self, it is no longer love. It becomes avoidance. Don't totally avoid your life in service to another.

CHAPTER TWO

The Bride Who Lost Her Voice

Without an early diagnosis or awareness of Asperger Syndrome (AS), many neurotypical (NT) spouses develop codependency, or adapt to the Aspie's counterproductive coping mechanisms by becoming overly responsible for everything that goes wrong in the relationship. In this chapter you will learn to challenge your own codependency so that you can make a transition to a healthier life.

Intuition Fails Without a Context

Many NTs tell me that they had a feeling at the start that something was not quite "right" in the relationship with their Aspie partner. But because they were having fun and fell in love and had so many interests in common, they ignored the subtle signals suggesting that a certain quality in the communication was unnerving. The flat affect, the rigid thinking, the child-like yes or no answers, while at first these seemed acceptable aspects of the Aspie partner's personality, they eventually make the NT realize that her sweetheart is not tracking another aspect of their relationship – all of those nonverbal cues that create the connection that goes deeper than words.

It is difficult to trust your intuition when the one you love acts as if your intuition is irrelevant. But intuition is what NTs are good at. Often NTs know something long before their consciousness can explain it. The problem with the early stage of a relationship between an Aspie and an NT is that the NT's intuition is working, but he or she has no reference point or context to explain the resulting feelings. If you don't know about Asperger's, how can you make sense of the missteps between you? Without this guide, many NTs become seriously depressed or even physically ill.

It Is the Meaning We Make of Life That Counts

Today I asked Helen to tell me more about her husband, Grant. I wanted to know how they met and decided to get married. Helen's quest for happiness and self-awareness is imbedded in the interaction of her past and present. She has made decisions and created interpretations and then developed beliefs based upon her life experiences with others, especially those she is close to.

NTs learn to know themselves in relationship with others, so as her therapist, it is important for me to know who these significant people are in Helen's life. If the actions and life path Helen has created are based upon faulty information or errors in judgment, I need to know the process she used so that I can help her change her focus and direction. As Helen weaves her story of being young and falling in love with Grant, I not only learn the facts of her life but also the meaning she is making of them.

I recognize that my fascination with Helen's life is more than professional. There is some kind of awakening going on inside of me as I listen to her telling one story after another. I have come to realize that Helen has no ordinary life and I can relate to that. We are a lot alike. I am eager to better understand the subtle intricacies of her life that have led her to this place of depression because it could be a breakthrough for me, too. How does depression take root in the lives of high-functioning people who appear to "have it all"? Are we spoiled?

There Is a Message in the Dream

Helen tells a story.

I awoke with a start, a terrible sinking feeling in my stomach. The dream was so real and frightening. I looked around the bedroom for reassurance. I noticed a little light was starting to creep through the window curtain, but it was still too early to get up. Next to me, Grant was sleeping peacefully, so I snuggled close to his warm body and tucked the covers close to make a tight cocoon around us. I felt better and drifted back to sleep.

Grant and I had decided to get married that night.

"So whadda ya think? Should we file a joint tax return next year?" he asked with a boyish grin.

"Oh, Grant, be serious. What are you saying?" Of course, I knew what he meant, but I had hoped he would make this moment more special, more romantic.

"Aw, you know what I'm saying. How about it?"

That was it! That's about as deep as Grant ever gets. Come to think of it, I don't remember Grant telling me he loved me. I knew he was enamored of me. I knew that he wanted to be with me all of the time. I loved him. And he made me laugh with his off-the-wall jokes and pranks. We had a lot in common. We were both well educated, liberal-minded, from good families, with a good start on building financial security. And we were both heading for graduate school to further our careers. Even though grad school would take its toll on our energies and our new marriage, we reasoned that we were up to the challenge because we had love and youth on our side.

But the dream that night was unnerving, and so was Grant's proposal. Although I loved him and thought marriage was a great idea, I had reservations. There was something I couldn't put my finger on. There was always something about Grant that was vaguely unnerving – not quite pleasant or unpleasant. It was that sliver in my mind again, the sliver that I "worried" but could never release.

When we discussed marriage over the next few days, I was excited but, oddly, I also resisted. Grant had no idea of how to plan a wedding. He seemed to expect that I would handle it. Considering that this was my second marriage, I hardly felt comfortable asking my parents for help again.

When I told Grant that I did not want to plan the wedding either, he decided to call his mother. He never asked about my reservations on getting married. He just accepted that it was time to ask his mother for help. And so it was settled. My future mother-in-law, whom I had never met, planned the wedding. Our only part was to fly in a couple of days before and show up at the church. Why was I so ambivalent about this marriage? Why couldn't I make more of a commitment? Why was it O.K. to get married if someone else arranged it for me?

The dream was very short, but I never forgot it: Grant tried to smother me with a pillow. I struggled, broke free and woke up. Was there a message in the dream? When I mentioned it to Grant, he just blew it off.

Reason Overcomes Intuition

Helen's story continues.

Over the next few months, Marcia, Grant's mother, handled everything for the wedding, including making reservations at our honeymoon hotel. She arranged the caterer, the banquet room, the flowers, the music, the photographer, the minister, the airline reservations, even the guests, all without consulting Grant or me. Grant and I did order wedding announcements. But considering that the wedding was to be out of state near his parents' home, few of my family and friends could attend. The announcements were mailed to family and friends more just to let them know that we were getting married. We decided to have a reception when we returned from our honeymoon, so that we could celebrate with our local family and friends.

I continued to resist the planning for our life together. Friends and coworkers held parties for us. There are photographs of the two of us smiling and opening well-wishers' cards and gifts. But I was becoming more and more anxious about the prospect of marrying Grant. In the meantime, he seemed oblivious of my anxieties. I tried to tell him about the dream, but he laughed it off. In fact, Grant is seldom interested in talking with me about anything meaningful. When he is happy, so should I be. That is his philosophy. So I try to rest in his reassurances.

Just before our wedding, we leased out Grant's home and he moved into mine. I was horrified, because he wanted to bring his junk into my house. He had ratty, old bachelor stuff that he prized and wanted to put in our living room. He never cleaned his house, so things were covered in layers of dust, grime and dog hair. He had three television sets and an old couch that smelled like dog. I insisted on a garage sale to get rid of anything that would sell and take the rest to the dump. But my resistance wasn't about Grant's stuff or poor taste in furnishings. I found that I didn't even want his old record albums on my shelves. Within reason, shouldn't I have been tolerant of his wishes and respected his right to bring some of his things to our new home?

I kept worrying about that sliver, but couldn't come up with a good reason not to marry Grant. I loved him. He was fun. I loved his quirky sense of humor, especially his Monty Python imitations. I reasoned that my intuitions were pre-wedding jitters. Perhaps I was just nervous about the change in lifestyle. I was twenty-seven, after all, and had established an adult life already. Maybe I was a little "set in my ways," "selfish" or "too independent." It would be good for me to learn to adapt to another person and not be so determined to have my way, I reasoned. So I put Grant's albums on my shelves.

But none of the reasoning I could come up with released the sliver. Those around me were happy for us and reassured me that it would all go well. They agreed that I was worrying over a transition. Change is difficult for all of us, even good changes. They suggested that I not hold myself back from happiness. I don't remember Grant taking any of my worries seriously. He went to work, watched TV and let time roll by.

Is Nurturing too Much to Ask For?

Helen continues.

I didn't have more nightmares, but a week before the wedding I contracted an upper-respiratory infection. The anxiety was definitely getting to me. But what bride has not had the jitters and come down with a cold just before her wedding? I shrugged it off and took some cold medicine. As the week wore on, I felt worse and worse. A fever developed, then a sore throat . . . a really sore throat. Soon I recognized the symptoms of a Strep infection.

"Grant, I think I am coming down with Strep throat."

"O.K.," he answered without any emotion.

"No really! I am not feeling very well. Maybe I should see a doctor."

"O.K.," Grant repeated in the same matter-of-fact way.

"Well, maybe I'll be better in a couple of days." I was giving up.

"O.K.," he said in his typical flat tone.

That's how it always is with Grant. I thought he was laid back, but now I realize that he just takes me at my word. He has no concept of what is going on with me. I wonder why I need validation from Grant to take care of myself. I am terribly independent when I am single, but immediately become terribly dependent in a relationship. That had to explain why I wanted Grant to "baby" me a bit about my sore throat. I probably believe that love means he should take me to the doctor or at least strongly suggest I go. I think he should tell me he is concerned. But then I must be too needy to want these things. A grown-up takes care of herself and doesn't need childish attention over a little illness. Still I kind of wish he would hug me and get me a glass of orange juice.

By the time we settled into our seats on the plane for the trip to Connecticut and our wedding, I had a pretty good fever developing and could hardly swallow. While Grant read his book, I slept, until the plane began decompressing for landing. The infection had spread into my Eustachian tubes, so the decompression made my head feel like it was going to explode. My ears were plugged. I couldn't swallow. I rocked back and forth to distract myself from the pain and kept wiggling my ears and blowing my nose to release the pressure. Nothing helped, and I was an exhausted mess when we landed. No point in explaining all of this to Grant because he wasn't sick and he would ignore me anyway unless I gave him explicit instructions on how to help me. I was simply too tired to explain.

When we got to the hotel where Marcia had made reservations, Grant busied himself with organizing his stuff. He always needs to fuss over his things. When traveling and staying at a hotel, I just put my bag in a corner, or hang up a few things, and then head out to explore. But Grant needs to make sure he has everything. He's obsessive.

He counted the bags several times and sorted through each bag to be sure that he hadn't forgotten anything. He then took out a pen, pencil, highlighter, sticky notes and his book, and began to read. We just arrived and my soon-to-be husband wants to study! I suppose it has to be dark to make love to your fiancée. Not that I was in great shape with the Strep infection any way, but I kind of hoped for a little romance, maybe a cuddle.

Time to Shut Down

Helen continues.

In the next couple of days, still feeling miserable, I met many of Grant's family members, all of whom seemed just like Grant. But it was hard for me to concentrate on them. I sat quietly in a corner and talked to no one, just watching his family buzz around. No one seemed to notice that I was not participating. No one asked about me. I guess they were busy with the wedding plans and parties. Grant seemed happy to be with his parents, and the three of them watched TV together from the dinner hour on to bedtime, while I slept fitfully on the couch.

The fever raged on, and the infection got so bad that I gagged. Finally, I told Grant I needed to find a doctor and get antibiotics or

I wouldn't be able to stand up at the wedding. So the day before the wedding, we found a doctor who confirmed my suspected diagnosis. By then I was dehydrated, unable to eat and had laryngitis. I was pleased that I had lost seven pounds, though. I would look like a Vogue *model in my wedding dress, with a nice pink flush from the fever.*

How I got through the wedding I will never know. It is a blur. I could not speak my vows very clearly. In fact, my words came out in a croaky whisper. Everyone laughed, thinking it was bridal nerves, but I knew I was shut down.

My first marriage was a disaster. I had been ambivalent on that wedding day, too. What was my reticence about this time? Grant is nothing like Bobby. My first marriage deteriorated due to Bobby's alcohol abuse. Grant, on the other hand, is smart, good looking, kind and gentle, and never abuses alcohol or drugs. But there is something wrong. The dream was so real. That was twenty years ago.

Is Love Living on Parallel Tracks?

Helen's intuition was obviously trying to break through to her, even on her wedding day, but she wouldn't listen. Why did she allow her rationalizations to override her common sense? I agree with Helen that Grant is hard to figure out. He seems like an affable fellow who is enjoying the wedding festivities. So he watches too much TV? Is that a crime?

But how could she ignore the dream? How could she ignore the illness that stole her voice? These are powerful metaphors of oppression. At a deep level, she knew that she was marrying someone who would take her "voice" away. An AS mate can do that. Grant was unaware of how Helen was feeling because he was not sick. Similarly, he didn't have the dream, so it was irrelevant. His inability to empathize left Helen to doubt herself. She thought that if Grant, and even his family, wasn't concerned about her illness, neither should she.

Little by little, Helen was being brainwashed into denying her own reality. When the man she loved acted as if she had nothing to worry about, Helen kept her worries to herself. But the worries didn't go away. They were not validated, so they could have no voice. I can imagine the screams of loneliness and injustice being stifled by the Strep infection.

But there had to be more. Why would a strong. intelligent woman put up with this insensitivity? Yes, Grant's charm was a good cover, but his lack of concern for Helen's health should not have been tolerated. And why didn't he ask her to explain the meaning of her dream? Why didn't he show some concern about her worries even if they were bridal jitters? Men are said to be obtuse about many things, but you would think that Grant would be more tuned into the woman he loved and planned to marry.

Those with Asperger Syndrome often cannot feel what is going on with another person unless they have had the same experience. And even then, they only know what *they* feel, not what their partner is feeling. They seem to run on a parallel track. Because it is parallel, women like Helen see the commonality between them and assume there is empathy. But this assumption is deadly. It set up Helen to believe she was understood when she was not. As long as Helen was willing to be there for Grant, he was happy, but he had no awareness of how to be there for her, nor was he able to notice that his empathy was missing.

In order to cope with this lack of empathy, Helen denied her own perceptions and feelings. On her wedding day, it was better to be the bride with no voice than to face the reality that something was "wrong" with Grant. It was too painful to accept that the man she loved and had chosen as her life partner might not be capable of knowing who she was.

So Helen chose the path that would lead her to denying more and more of her personal experience in favor of Grant's model of reality. No wonder she was depressed. She had accepted that love and marriage meant living on parallel tracks, never connecting. How could she live like this trying to love a man who does not really love back?

Lessons Learned

1. Trust your intuition. If the situation seems crazy, maybe it is. This statement is worth repeating from Chapter One.
2. Consistency is a virtue, but being irrationally consistent is co-dependency. Never compromise on your beliefs or values if your intuition tells you to hold fast.
3. If your Asperger loved one does not understand you, stop right there. Explain yourself in simple, concrete detail and ask for what you want or need – in simple, concrete detail. Aspies cannot read your mind.
4. Never expect your AS loved one to be like you. He or she will fail you. You will feel demoralized unless you can come to terms with your loved one's Asperger Syndrome.
5. Appreciate your AS loved one for what he or she can offer, such as a sense of humor, instead of grieving over what is lacking.

CHAPTER THREE

Living in a War Zone

Living in a war zone is an apt metaphor to describe living with the tortuous anxieties and "meltdowns" that many Aspie loved ones go through. In addition to her husband, Helen not only carries the burden of caring for her Aspie daughter (Jasmine) during these times, but also of having to create a safe environment for Jason, her neurotypical (NT) son. Helen copes by avoiding self-care and learning to shut down emotionally. In this chapter you will be encouraged to assess whether you have shut down too and get some tips on how to reawaken yourself.

Looking for a Psychological Bunker to Hide In

Is it domestic violence? Shell shock? Survivor stress? Depression? Until the general public had access to information about Asperger Syndrome (AS), the distress that NTs struggled with was hard to diagnose. Depression and anxiety were the common diagnoses, since patients demonstrated symptoms of those disorders. Talk therapies and modern SSRI (selective serotonin reuptake inhibitors – popular type of antidepressant) drugs like Prozac helped, but the burden was still on the individual with the symptom. What was missing was a social context for the development of the NT's depression and anxiety.

Once you begin to understand the problematic communication that erupts when living with an Aspie, or the co-dependency that emerges when an NT tries to cope with the irrational temper tantrums of an Aspie loved one, it is much easier to understand why family members of Aspies start looking like they are living in a war zone. There are no mortars raining down on them. There are no scenes of horror to witness. No one is frightened for his or her life or personal safety. Nevertheless, the daily confusing missteps are like little static electric shocks – dozens of them. And these shocks leave NTs feeling like they want to crawl into a bunker and hide.

Shell Shock

Helen looked a bit more subdued than usual today. She always has that look on her face – intense, concerned and even a bit suspicious, as if she is waiting for the other shoe to drop. Although she is a beautiful woman, the energy behind her beauty is trapped somewhere deep inside, glowing ever so faintly, as if held hostage behind a thick wall of cold marble. Every hair in place, well dressed, manicured nails, yet the radiance is missing.

Where is the life? I am beginning to think that this has some of the characteristics of post-traumatic stress disorder (PTSD), or what they called shell shock in World War I. But Helen has not lived through a war, nor has she survived a major personal tragedy such as a rape or a house fire, often the causes of PTSD. Her life has had its ups and downs, to be sure, but the typical PTSD crises that would explain her tentativeness, hyper-vigilance and psychological numbing – those crises are not known to me, if they exist at all.

I continue to work that sliver in my own mind. Things just don't add up. Is she hiding things from me or is this woman just very unusual? Is she wired differently? I have spent many months with Helen, but I still feel as if I will never know her. Perhaps that is how she feels, too – that no one will ever know her. That would be sad. Locked forever in a prison of translucent marble.

As Helen tells me today's story about a recent incident with her children, Jasmine who is diagnosed with AS and Jason who is neurotypical, I appreciate the incredible strength she has for survival even if trapped in her marble bunker.

The Bonds of Survivor Stress

Helen weaves another story.

As he reached the top of the stairs, Jason leaned his back against the wall where the coats hang on a rack by the door. With resignation, he slowly slid to the floor. I was taking a load of clothes to the laundry room, but put down my basket immediately and went over to him. He looked so small, with the coats hanging over his head and his face resting in his cupped hands. He was sobbing quietly, and I wasn't sure if he wanted to be disturbed. Boys can be like that, you know, especially at fourteen. I didn't want to ruffle his manhood.

Still I couldn't bear to leave my son suffering like that, so I bent down and sat next to him on the floor under the coats. He let me put my arm around him, and I pushed the hair back from his forehead, stroking his dear little face with my hand. He looks so much like his father, but is nothing like him. Jason and I are close. We can talk like best friends.

"Honey, what's wrong?" I finally asked.

In one breathless explosion of feeling, he said, "I hate my sister!"

Jason looked at me, not with a look of anger but one of utter desperation and also a little fear of disapproval from me for what he had just said. Hatred is not the kind of thing this gentle boy feels. He is loving and kind, and has dozens of friends. Even when he was a baby, people would come up to me and remark about his incredible and engaging smile. Jason is one of those people you want to be around. I may be his mother, but once you meet him, you will see what I mean. He's a doll!

As Helen talked about Jason, I couldn't help but notice the contradiction between mother and son. Helen is the woman held emotional hostage behind cold marble, yet she describes her son as this warm and engaging soul. How could these two people be in the same family? How could they possibly relate to each other? And yet she has a very strong bond with her son. They do seem to know each other in ways that escape others.

Helen continues her story.

I hate to admit it, but I understood what Jason meant when he told me he hated his sister. When you are constantly walking on eggshells around Grant and Jasmine, you just want to scream some days. Loving them is not enough for either Jasmine or her dad. They are always demanding more.

"Jasmine is not very easy to live with, Jason," I conceded. He looked up at me with a sense of relief in his eyes upon hearing that I know how he feels. He feels guilty about how he feels, but he can't help it. Jasmine drives him to it.

"Dad and Jasmine need a special kind of handling. It is best to leave them alone when they start accusing you of things you did not do. Come to me if Jasmine is getting too difficult for you."

That's what I usually say to Jason when he has these experiences. I decided a long time ago that I didn't want to contribute to his feelings of being misunderstood by denying that there is something wrong with my daughter and husband. They don't think like other people. They are demanding and hurtful. They scream at you for no reason and then act as if it is justifiable to scream because they are distressed. There are times when Jasmine flips out and twists everything you say, accusing you of wrongdoing because of some imagined slight. As Jasmine has grown, this paranoid, delusional behavior has escalated. At fourteen, even though she is Jason's twin, they are nothing alike. As outgoing, engaging and loving as Jason is, his sister is a loner and eccentric and self-absorbed like her father. It is so odd. How did this happen to our family?

"But Mom, I do come to you, and sometimes you tell me to take care of it myself. Besides, everything happened so fast. All I did was ask

Jasmine if I could use the Xbox, and she flipped out on me and tried to claw my face. Honest, I didn't call her a name or anything. She just came after me."

At this point, Jasmine came running into the kitchen and found us talking on the stairs. She was livid and immediately confronted me. "You always take his side! You should do something about him! You never discipline him. Punish him! Punish him for once. Take a stand. You are such a loser for a mother. You let him have everything he wants and don't care about me at all."

Trying to be patient with her, I said, "Jasmine, honey, I love you both. You know that. What happened? Why are you upset? Tell me about it. I will listen."

But Jasmine continued to rage. "You know good and well why I am upset. Punish him. None of this grounding stuff that he always gets away with. Punish him. Make him mind. He is worthless and so are you."

"Jasmine, you are so upset. There must be something that is bothering you. What could it be? What did Jason do?" I tried to keep myself calm to help her calm down.

But Jasmine was on a roll. "Just punish him. And stop looking at me that way. Both of you. Stop it, or I will make you stop. You are both disgusting."

By now Jasmine was screaming at the top of her lungs. The tirade went on for another twenty minutes. No amount of soothing her helped. When I asked Jason to go to his room so Jasmine and I could be alone, Jasmine got angrier.

"He's not going anywhere. You need to punish him. If he leaves this room, you'll be sorry."

At this pronouncement, Jasmine lifted her fist in a menacing manner and aimed for my face. She does this a lot but has never hit me. She has come up behind me and tried to choke me and she has hit me in the back with her fist. But it was not very hard. It was more like she couldn't express herself any other way. And I know she counts on me so much to make things work for her that when I fail she blames me for her life of loneliness, confusion and terror.

I tried another tack. "O.K., Jasmine. Jason can stay here. What should I punish him for?"

But Jasmine was not fooled. "You are just trying to fool me. You are not going to punish him. You are just trying to get me to stop being angry. I know what you are up to. Get out of my sight. You make me sick."

"O.K., Jasmine, we'll leave. Why don't you fix yourself something to eat. Jason and I will go to my office and work on his homework. When you want to talk some more, just let me know."

With a look of hatred in her eyes, Jasmine said, "Oh, like you care! I could slit my throat and you would do nothing. What kind of mother are you anyway? And that little snot with you is just as bad." A new wave of anger ripped across her face. "Stop smirking. Stop whispering to each other. STOP IT!!!! NOWWWWW!" she screams as long and as loudly as she can.

By then Jason and I were so tired of the tantrum that we were getting rummy. You know how it is when, no matter how weird or even dangerous a situation is, you just feel like laughing. I looked at him and he looked back, and we smiled a tiny little knowing smile that we hoped Jasmine did not see. We both knew it was craziness and that it would last for a couple of hours. So we settled in for the siege.

I asked Helen where Grant was during all of this, and without skipping a beat, she told me he was sitting in front of the computer in the family room, oblivious of the commotion. It never occurred to her to ask him for help. Helen, long ago, learned not to ask Grant for help with the children because he would get as angry as Jasmine. Then she and Jason would have two people after them. And when Grant throws a fit, Jasmine is uncontrollable for hours. So Helen just tries to take care of these times on her own. She and Jason just hunker down and wait it all out, like taking cover in a bunker in a war zone until the bombing stops.

Survivors Are Alone

Living with an Asperger's mate like Grant and an Asperger's teenager like Jasmine can be like living in a war zone. Helen and her son never know when or where the emotional bombs will explode next. They also have no defense, except each other. They are veterans of a war that has been going on in their home for years. That is their bond, the kind of bond that comes from having no one else to cling to when you are faced daily with fighting for your psychological life.

Jason has not let go of his exuberance for life yet. He rests in the comfort and strength of his mother's compassion, believing that some day he won't have to live like this. Helen loves him, and that makes all of the difference in his survival under the daunting verbal abuse of his sister and father.

But who is there for Helen? Her fourteen-year-old son needs her love and protection, so Helen cannot lean on him. Who does Helen lean on? No wonder she is hiding behind that beautiful but thick wall of marble. It is safe in there.

I want to help Helen come alive again. I can imagine this graceful woman as a young girl, full of creativity and dreams, just like Jason. She is strong and compassionate and daily works not only for the welfare of her children but for her patients as a naturopathic physician. But is all of that nurturing just another way she keeps herself locked up? If she turned that healing power on herself and came more fully alive, how could she endure the abuse? Would she have to make a choice between herself and her family? And if she chose herself, could she stand the grief and the guilt?

We don't know, and for now Helen feels safer as a hostage behind that translucent marble wall that allows her to be there for others, if not for herself.

Lessons Learned

1. This is abuse. This is mind-numbing abuse, and the natural response is to shut down so that you don't feel the pain.
2. If you choose to get better, you must put yourself first. Do not tolerate abuse.
3. Seek professional help from a psychologist who knows how to treat PTSD and similar conditions. Even if that is not the correct diagnosis, many of the effects fit your situation.
4. Go very slowly. It is not easy to extricate yourself from an abusive relationship. It takes time to understand the dysfunction, and it takes time to heal and resurrect your life.

CHAPTER FOUR

Making It Through the Night

Even as Helen handles the nightmarish outbursts of her daughter, Jasmine, and the lack of parenting support from her Asperger (AS) husband, Grant, she is able to enjoy the good times with her loved ones. This little bit of joy helps her carry on.

In this chapter you should start to get the idea that detachment is the answer. Whether by turning your life over to a higher power (God, Spirit, or the Source), or by letting go of your preconceived notions of the way love and family life should be, detachment keeps you sane.

Reclaim Your Sanity by Detaching

If a neurotypical (NT) acts as if she has shell shock, the extreme anxieties and obsessive-compulsive nature of the Aspie loved one can be equally as devastating to live with. Anxiety is common for those with AS. Whether it is a hard-wiring issue or the result of years of frustration dealing with a primarily NT world, those with Asperger Syndrome seem to be powder kegs waiting to explode . . . or implode. They don't always act out against their loved ones. Very often Aspies' distress manifests as self-mutilating behaviors such as cutting off chunks of their hair or picking at their fingers until they bleed. I even knew one young woman who would repeatedly stick straight pins into her scalp until she reached the bone. Her mother would hide the sewing implements, only later to find them stashed in a drawer in her daughter's room.

If NTs and Aspies are to work together to reclaim their sanity and establish a healthy relationship, they must understand how to detach. It is not easy for an NT mother to detach when she discovers that her daughter is sticking pins in her head, but that is exactly what she must do to fully accept the world of her Aspie child. Detachment is letting go of preconceived notions of how something should be and working with what you have. Then when you finally get one of those little lovable golden moments of connection, it is all the more precious.

The Pain of No Connection

Helen continues her story of Jasmine's meltdown.

Finally, Jasmine was willing to let Jason slip away to bed at about eleven o'clock. She was getting so tired herself that she could not keep the tirade going. However, she was not willing to let me be. I remained her hostage for another hour or so. She continued to accuse me of being the worst creature on the planet, and her verbal abuse had escalated to very foul language. She refused to go to her room. She refused to take any medication that might calm her down. She followed me wherever I went, refusing to let me out of her sight.

After tantrumming for hours, she finally slumped down onto the stairs, just a few feet away from where Jason had earlier sat under the coat rack. She was exhausted. The wild look in her eyes was gone, replaced by fear and deep, deep hurt. She had been crying so hard that snot was streaming down her face and dripping onto the floor. Her hair was wet with perspiration. And the body odor was strong, that distinctive smell stemming from infrequent showering and the manic episode coursing through her body.

She finally let me come close to her and put my arm around her. "Sweetie, it's time to go to bed and get some rest. You have school tomorrow. Would you like a Zanax to help you sleep?"

We have had to try a huge variety of psychiatric medications because nothing else will work. Her psychiatrist thinks she may be bipolar as well as Asperger's, but who knows? Whatever it is, it is a nightmare for her to live with it, and it is a nightmare to live with her.

"Why don't you just kill me?" Jasmine asked, looking at me seriously. She says this sometimes after a manic episode like this. "Why don't you just kill me? If you were a good mother, you would not make me suffer any more. I am useless. I have no life. I will never have a life. I can't do anything right. I just blow up and make a mess of things."

My heart is breaking for her when she talks like this. "I love you Jasmine. I am here for you, and we will find a way to get through this together. There has to be an answer. We just haven't found it yet."

"Just kill me. Then you wouldn't have to work so hard. And you wouldn't fight with dad. And you and Jason could have a life. You like him better any way."

I had to find a way to break up this depression, but I feel so helpless when she talks like this.

"Jasmine. You are my only daughter. You are bright and creative, and I know that you will make a big contribution to the world when you grow up. You are so sensitive that you take things very hard. Let me give you a Zanax so you can sleep. I will cuddle you and we can fall asleep together. Let's go to the bathroom and I will wash your face."

Like a little child, she fell into my arms, and I half carried her to the bathroom, even though she is almost as big as me. I took a washcloth with cool water and wiped the tears and mucous from her face. I washed her hands. Then I got a cup of water and her pill. She cooperated, thank God! The tantrum was over. I asked her if she was hungry but she just wanted to lie down and try to sleep.

Jasmine was starting to feel remorseful. "Jason will hate me tomorrow. I can't live like this."

"Jason won't hate you, honey," I said. "He is a good brother. He admires you. He knows you have bad times like this and that it is not

about him. He is a brother after all and will get angry with you, but he will always love you. Don't forget that love is very strong and very important. Now let's put on your pajamas, and I will curl up with you until you fall asleep."

It didn't take long for the Zanax to take effect, and soon Jasmine was sleeping quietly, though it was hard for her to breathe because she was all stuffed up from all of the crying and screaming. I hoped that she would not have a headache in the morning.

By now it was about 2 a.m. I stumbled to my room to try to get a little rest before work the next day. Grant was asleep. When I came in, he stirred a bit and asked how things were going. "Is Jasmine O.K.? Things seemed pretty hot and heavy there for a while."

"Yes, Grant. She's O.K. The kids had a fight, and it was hard for Jasmine to settle down. Do you know that it is 2 a.m.?"

"Wow, is it that late?" he said. "Well, I am glad that everything is O.K. Hope you get some sleep. You deserve it. 'Night, honey." Then he rolled over without a kiss or hug and went to sleep.

These moments of disconnect are so difficult for me. Once again Grant was aware that there was a problem, but he can tune out the screaming while he sits in front of the computer or television. He says things that make me think he understands, but then he isn't very deep. I know that he cares and that he loves me in his own way, but it is so strange that he treats these things with Jasmine as if they are minor. Since he wasn't bothered and I took care of everything, I guess he thinks it's over. But it isn't over. I did not really sleep all night. I am so frightened for Jasmine.

Surrender to Survive

When Helen finished her story, I was drained. How could one woman put up with all of this? She gets no sleep and no support from her husband. She is terrorized by her daughter, whom she loves deeply. Her heart is broken because she cannot help one of the most precious people in her life, Jasmine. And she sometimes feels she is letting Jason down.

I let Helen know that I am amazed at her strength. I tell her that her children are lucky to have her. I tell her that if anyone can help Jasmine find the answers, it is Helen. I tell her that Jason will grow up to be a remarkable man, with his mother setting the example for courage and compassion. I tell her that it isn't fair she has to handle all of this, but that there has to be a greater purpose. I tell her that each of us has our own challenges. Jasmine has hers and Helen has hers.

Helen continues.

Oh, I know that God has a reason for all of this. I try to remind myself that my burdens are no greater than another's. I keep working on surrender, you know, accepting that God is in charge and will guide me to the next step. It isn't easy when the children are hurting so much and Grant is a space cadet. And even if God doesn't really care about my problems, I am still given an opportunity to grow through all of this. But I wish I had more answers. I am so tired.

You know, Jasmine is at the edge of giving up entirely. And she is only fourteen. She refuses to shower and brush her teeth, sometimes for days. When I was doing the laundry, I noticed that she hasn't been using toilet paper again. I thought I had solved that problem. The last time she stopped using toilet paper, she told me she didn't have the time to wipe. Can you imagine?

And she hoards things – odd things, like little balls of lint. And I found chunks of her hair cut and tied up and stored in her bureau. She digs at her scalp until the skin bleeds. When she was younger, she would shred her clothing and her blankets, one thread at a time, but she has stopped that. She is so miserable. I guess these odd little self-destructive behaviors bring her some kind of comfort.

Again I am dumbstruck. I know that Jasmine is seeing a psychiatrist. But when is this child going to get some relief? She's fourteen, going on fifteen. She has no friends, no outside interests. She lives in her room, seemingly content with hiding out from the world and absorbed in the Internet. Like Grant, she has little need for others, and the computer provides enough stimulation for her to make it through each day.

Brief Moments of Joy

I can't stand the sad stories any more for today and ask Helen to talk about times when she and Jasmine or Jason, or both, experience joyful times. I don't dare ask about Grant.

Helen's face brightens up as she shares this anecdote.

Of course. There have been some wonderful moments. We like to feed the seagulls at the beach. It's a tradition each time we head to the ocean. One time the seagulls were very aggressive and dive-bombed the kids because they would not wait until they let go of the bread crumbs. Jasmine turned around and threw the bread into the wind, and it was blown back into her hair. The seagulls came after her. She ran, but she wasn't frightened. She just thought it was wild! We all laughed. We tell that story each time we go to the beach.

Then there was this time at Christmas when Jasmine told me that one of my new Christmas decorations was broken. I had bought a mechanical bird that chirped when you pressed one button and sang Christmas songs when you pressed the other. It's a cardinal, and it's little head moves from side to side as it sings. Actually Jasmine didn't say the bird was broken, she said, "Something's wrong with your new bird, Mom."

So I came into the living room to see what she was talking about. I pressed the buttons and it all worked just fine. "I don't see anything wrong with the bird. What do you mean, Jasmine?"

"Well, Mom, this bird is a cardinal, right?"

"Right," I said.

"And male cardinals are red and the females are kind of brownish," Jasmine continued.

"Well, I guess so." I was kind of puzzled about the direction this was going in.

"Gosh, Mom. This fake bird is red but sings Christmas songs with a female voice!" Jasmine looked matter-of-fact.

I was so astonished that at eleven or twelve, she was making this distinction. But that's Jasmine for you. And it was not a joke to her. She was dead serious. So I smiled and said, "Well you know, honey, it's more Christmassy if the bird is red, but we should let the people at the store know this little distinction. They might think it is funny. You are so clever to notice these things." Jasmine smiled at the praise.

When she smiles I know that she is comfortable and will not rage if I criticize her. So I pressed on with another observation. "Perhaps we can tell everyone that we have a hermaphrodite Christmas songbird!" She turned to me and laughed out loud. She got the joke, and she was pleased that she helped set it up. So that's what we call the bird each year when we decorate the house. And we let everyone know who visits that we are not bigots because we have decorations for all genders.

Are a Few Moments of Joy Enough?

At one moment, the anguish that this woman feels is too much for me to bear. At another moment, her life seems delightfully bohemian. What a contrast. This must be what it is like to live with people whose thinking is disconnected, such as those with Asperger Syndrome. At one moment they take offense when none is suggested. At another, their brains can connect the oddest things and make us laugh. These creative minds are incredible, yet so unable to connect on many small intimate details of life. Helen must get joy from those moments when Jasmine and Grant startle her with their unconventional thinking. But is this enough to endure all those hours when she is the object of their abuse?

I wonder about the bonds this family shares. It is clear that Helen loves them all. That is a good thing. That makes her strong. But the love is not returned in a way that nurtures Helen. No comfort or hugs from Grant when she has spent hours with a raging teenager. No support from the psychiatrist – well not yet any way. Even Jason's love makes Helen feel guilty since she cannot protect him from the Aspie outbursts of Grant or Jasmine. There are just a few joyful moments when Helen can give love to her children between the conflicts – this is sounding more and more like a war zone to me, and under these circumstances, who wouldn't feel close to going over the edge?

Lessons Learned

1. Detach from making meaning of everything. Everything that is happening is "just so." Learn to accept the facts as they are instead of making meaning of everything. If you grieve and carry on, you keep the problems alive.
2. People with Asperger's suffer immensely. If they are willing, make sure they receive professional guidance (psychotherapy, support groups, educational groups and social skill building classes) rather than allowing them to rely solely on your love and support. If you are all they have, they can develop resentment toward you for failing to save them.
3. Turn over your problems to a higher power (God, your Higher Power, Spirit, or the Source) because they are beyond you. Seek support and psychotherapy for yourself as well.
4. You cannot "cure" Asperger Syndrome, so focus on what you can do and appreciate and enjoy your life.
5. Remember to be there for those NT family members who also need your love and can return it. If you focus all of your attention on the Aspies, you are letting down the ones who can co-create a reciprocal and loving relationship.
6. Recite the Serenity Prayer. It has helped countless codependents recover.

   God grant me the serenity
   To accept the things I cannot change;
   Courage to change the things I can;
   And the wisdom to know the difference.

CHAPTER FIVE

Being There, or Being Present

While Aspies are content with *being there*, neurotypicals (NTs) want their partners to *be present*. Grant demonstrates those little annoying behaviors that, day after day, lead so many NTs to want to scream. Some have called it water torture, because the constant little drips of annoying disconnecting behaviors eventually mount up.

This chapter may help you recognize that the anger you feel is perfectly normal. However, it is not useful, and it is important not to let the anger get the best of you. In this chapter Helen learns how to stand up for herself and gains some insight into her husband's distractible Aspie thinking and lack of emotional connection. This insight helps create detachment, even though Helen continues to vacillate between co-dependency and anger for a while.

Detach from the Distractible Aspie

With a context for shell shock, and a method for coping with the daily oppression, as we discussed in the previous chapters, it is time to take back your life. Detachment makes it easier. It's not that you stop loving your Aspie partner. It's that you remain true to yourself instead of accommodating to Aspie thinking when it doesn't suit you. Sarcasm and contempt are destructive forms of anger. If you find that you are becoming angry, rather than detached, you are not truly letting go and accepting the reality as you have it.

Finding Humor

Helen's mood was pretty upbeat the last couple of sessions. She and Grant were planning a vacation, a cruise to Mexico. The children were going along, but Helen was also looking forward to some time reconnecting with Grant, even hoping for a little romance. The cruise was one of those family ships with plenty for teens to do while their parents explored more mature options.

In truth, Helen was putting the whole trip together without Grant's help. Grant was busy with his work as a software engineer. He seems to be a workaholic. Helen heard all of the time about how stressful his career was and that she couldn't expect him to help with very much at home. Whenever Helen asked for help in the kitchen or the yard, or with the children, Grant would snap at her and say, "I have to work and you don't seem to understand. I can't help it. My job is very demanding. My time is not my own, you know. I'm a manager, and my boss and employees count on me. They have to come first."

It seemed strange the first time Helen told me this about Grant. After all, she is a professional too and works long hours. Her patients depend on her. She has emergency calls. Yet, she is able to put aside time for Grant and the twins. She is the one to register the kids for soccer or seek out the perfect piano teacher. She is the one who makes sure the freezer is stocked with food. Does Grant really believe his work is more demanding than Helen's? Does he really believe that Helen should handle a full-time career and everything else in their lives too, such as managing the household and the children?

Many dual-career couples face this type of inequity at home, but there is something strange about Grant's assumptions, at least as laid out to me by Helen. Other dual-career husbands acknowledge that their wives do a lot. In fact, most admit that their wives do more than they do at home. They pitch in, to be sure, but survey after survey has found that career women still do more work at home than their spouses.

But in Grant's case, there is no recognition that his wife takes care of all of these things. And he seems oblivious of how ridiculous his statement sounds . . . that his work comes first. Grant sounds a lot like Archie Bunker in the 70s TV show, and we all used to laugh at Archie's self-centeredness and root for Edith when she occasionally pulled one over on him.

Helen shares an anecdote.

You know, Grant thinks he's a good dad because he attends the soccer games and piano recitals. But in reality, he always brings his laptop and work along. Sometimes he is so self-absorbed that he misses the play or the moment when Jason scores. I've pointed out to him that none of the other parents bring their work to a soccer game, but Grant only reminds me that I just don't understand. He's a very important man, you know!

I detected a hint of sarcasm in her voice when Helen made that last comment. And then one of those rare Mona Lisa smiles crept across her face. Helen is intriguing. She is so lonesome in this lackluster marriage, but she does have a sense of humor. Probably another of her survival techniques – to see the humor in what she finds herself unable to change.

Being Reasonable Doesn't Work

Helen shares another anecdote.

Last fall I asked Grant to look at his schedule to help me plan this cruise. I like to get things organized early so we can put the money aside and get the best deals on airfare and things like that, you know? We could go either in the spring or in the fall. I asked him when he

thought he could get vacation time. He wasn't sure. There were some big projects coming up, he said. He was going to have to take a trip to India and maybe Spain, all for the company. He just wasn't sure he could break away for a cruise. Work is very important to Grant, you know." [There was that sarcastic tone and wry smile again.]

Other people take vacations. I'm sure his boss would let him take one. I tried to get Grant to be reasonable, but whenever I get reasonable, he comes up with some other excuse. This time he told me it was too expensive. Vacations are expensive, I countered. Besides, this one was a family one, and I could get pretty good rates planning this far ahead. But I couldn't make a sale. It's like Grant understands his work very well, but he doesn't have a clue about how to relate to me or the kids. He loves us, but we are a mystery to him. He finds it odd that we would like a vacation!

So I got tired of waiting for Grant to wake up and help plan a vacation. It is so depressing to get his putdowns and putoffs. I would like, just once, for Grant to put me and the kids first. But that'll be the day! So I decided to plan the cruise without him. I picked the dates, made reservations, bought airline tickets . . . for the three of us! Then I wrote Grant the following note and left it on his desk.

At that point Helen pulled out a copy of the letter she had written to Grant and handed it to me.

Dear Grant,
Jasmine, Jason and I are taking a cruise to Mexico in October. It's a short three-day cruise, but I thought the kids would enjoy Disneyland so I added that on. We'll be gone for ten days. We would love to have you join us if you can break away from work. I have enclosed the itinerary so that you can make your own reservations.
Love,
Helen

Waiting for Her Husband to Grow Up

I was pleased that Helen was getting more assertive with Grant, instead of coping, accommodating and getting frustrated. It was time that she started having a life. Grant decided to join them for the trip after all, although he asked Helen to make the reservations for him. But even with this positive step, living with Grant seems so much work for Helen. He seems so obtuse, so narcissistic-like.

What does Helen see in him? But that isn't a fair question, I suppose. I don't know Grant very well. In fact, I only met him once, when he brought Helen to an appointment because her car was in the shop.

Helen introduced Grant to me at that time. It was an unremarkable meeting except that I noticed that Grant seemed a bit immature. He made some comment that he was glad his wife had a "good shrink" because she seemed to need someone to talk to. He seemed totally unaware that his wife is hurting and that she might like to talk with him, not me. I wonder if Grant lives in a childlike world where everything is just fine if the grownups take care of the hard stuff. Since Helen had me to talk with, Grant didn't need to relate to her other than in a superficial way. That's how it seems to me. I think Helen must have fallen in love with Grant's boyishness and has been waiting ever since for him to grow up and be a husband.

An Altered Reality

To my surprise, Grant was waiting for Helen today when I opened the door to show her out after our session. She hadn't told me that he was coming to pick her up.

Grant stepped up close to me and said, "Hey, doc. Did you know you're going to miss Helen the next couple of sessions? I'm taking her on a cruise to Mexico. It's a long time coming. Should have done this a long time ago for her. It's about time she got a little R and R, don't you think?"

I was speechless. Either Helen had misled me, or Grant was taking credit for this vacation and also acting as if he was concerned for her welfare. Helen interrupted before I could say a word. Spotting the confused look on my face, she stepped in to explain.

"Oh, I'm sorry. I didn't explain to you everything about the trip. Grant is so busy and he has wanted a family trip for some time, but he just couldn't find the time to arrange it. So I made a few phone calls, and it all came together. It's a wonderful opportunity for all of us to get some rest and relaxation. Grant works so hard and such long hours. I am very pleased that he can break away for this trip."

Grant stood there smiling at me, smiling at his wife and acting like this all made sense. Helen is so used to covering for Grant that she momentarily forgot who she was making apologies to. She has spent months describing to me her painfully lonely and oppressive marriage, and all of a sudden, without batting an eyelash, she co-dependently stepped right in and kept the system alive with a white lie about the upcoming vacation.

Helen looked at me and smiled the same simple smile that I saw on Grant's face. I guess this kind of thing is usual for them both, and I suppose that most people believe them. But I don't believe it for a moment. That sliver in my mind keeps worrying me. What are these contradictions telling me?

Helen is so clear about her dissatisfaction with their marriage. She complains about Grant's lack of attentiveness. Their intimate life is at a standstill and has been for years. Grant does not seem to need physical affection or conversation, or even the occasional smile between sweethearts. Helen is capable of calling him on the lack of followthrough for a family vacation, and yet when put to the test, she crumbles and accepts the craziness. Is she conscious of this? Is she embarrassed for Grant's immaturity? Or does she step into some altered state of reality when dealing with Grant?

An altered reality . . . that makes the sliver in my mind wriggle loose a bit more. Could Helen somehow slip into an altered state when faced with Grant's incongruities, especially when juxtaposed with a third person's reality? For example, Helen tells me often how annoying it is when Grant brings the newspaper into a restaurant and reads during the entire meal rather than talk with her. As rude as this may be, it is even more disconcerting to her when they are entertaining guests and Grant chooses to play on his Palm Pilot instead of joining the conversation. When Helen asks Grant to put away his PDA, his typical reply is "What? I'm listening," because he apparently has no awareness that being present means more than being there physically.

Helen is aware of this immature behavior because she goes so far as to ask him to put away the newspaper or his PDA and to join their guests. But just now, she allowed Grant to get away with taking credit for the vacation. Why? Perhaps she is desperate for the kind of life she is willing to lie about.

Lessons Learned

1. Anger is a signal that there is something you should pay attention to. You ignore this signal at your peril.
2. Those with AS are very distractible, just like those with attention deficit disorder (ADD). Don't take it personally that they have a hard time focusing on you. But be firm and let them know you want their attention . . . NOW.
3. Stop waiting for your AS loved one to join you in life. If he or she isn't interested, go do your life any way.
4. Don't ever excuse unconscionable behavior. That leads to codependency and failure.

CHAPTER SIX

Sex Is Not a Commodity

In this chapter, we meet Monique, who cracks open the delicate topic of sex and intimacy between a neurotypical (NT) and an Aspie. Many, many couples have trouble in this department. If you think about it, it makes sense. Aspies have trouble relating to the nonverbal communication in relationships, and sex is about as nonverbal as it gets.

In this chapter you will learn how to use the tools from other chapters to revitalize your sex life. But don't expect perfection, please! The NT may have to give up his or her dream of deepening passion in the bedroom in exchange for the intellectual acceptance that the Aspie partner does have love and respect.

Don't Live Life in the Deep Freeze

Sex is one of those topics that deserves a book of its own, especially in the context of NT-Aspie relationships. If communication about ordinary everyday subjects is difficult between these folks, just imagine the dicey situation of pillow talk gone haywire. The concrete thinking, distractibility and mind blindness of the Aspie juxtaposed with the intuitions and nonverbals and the metaphorical language of the NT creates a whole other universe of problems in the bedroom.

After repeated failure to meet NT expectations, performance anxiety goes through the roof for most Aspies, and they turn away from their loved ones in self-protection. It is not rejection but self-preservation. Many give up and live life in the love deep freeze . . . or seek other alternatives. However, if you desire to improve this aspect of your marriage, the bottom line is that NTs must take charge in the bedroom. In order for intimacy to blossom, you need to keep an open mind, be compassionate and guide your Aspie loved one's every move.

Getting Ready to Talk About S.E.X.

Monique was being very tentative today. Normally a very outgoing woman who launches into our sessions with an amusing quip about some event from the week, today she seemed to need prompting to get to the root of her concerns.

Monique is in her late thirties and, as I said, very outgoing – a vivacious and petite blonde. She married Sebastian, four years her junior, after a disastrous first marriage to an alcoholic. She and Sebastian have a son, Jacque, age three, who is the light of their lives. To adapt to Sebastian's budding career as a university math professor, Monique quit her job and happily stays home with their toddler. At least she was happy for a while. Now there is a growing unrest in her marriage.

Sebastian and Monique were married on the fly, so to speak, after Monique discovered she was pregnant. Being an older first-time mom, Monique was thrilled about the pregnancy but not so sure about the marriage. Now three years later, she comes to my office weekly to find ways to deal with the problems that have emerged in such a short time of marriage to a brilliant man with Asperger Syndrome (AS).

Sebastian has been a cooperative patient. He unabashedly acknowledges his Aspie ways and even points out others in his profession who have similar characteristics. In fact, Tony Attwood[1] and others have referred to universities as "sheltered workshops" for professors with AS.

Unfortunately, progress in therapy is slow for both Monique and Sebastian. Because of Sebastian's busy class schedule, student

[1]Internationally known expert on autism spectrum disorders. www.tonyattwood.com/au

advising load and research, he seldom attends therapy with his wife. So Monique is learning to adapt to Sebastian in more ways than one. But she is getting tired and demoralized.

"Monique, you seem pretty quiet today. Is there something on your mind?"

"Yes, Dr. Marshack, but I don't quite know how to say it. I mean, it is kind of embarrassing. You know I love Sebastian even though he drives me crazy every day with his Aspie ways! But since you have explained that he is really a good soul, I try to translate."

"Yes, of course, you love him. That's why you're here. Trying to learn new ways of communicating past those NT-Aspie barriers. But has something new come up?" I know how hard it is for Monique to talk about many things because she does not always have the words to describe the unusual in a relationship with an Asperger mate.

Monique slowly reveals her concern. "Well, it's not new really. It's about sex. You have never asked me before about our sex life, so I don't know if I can talk with you about it." Monique looks at me with inquiring eyes, searching my face for approval, something she has a hard time getting from Sebastian.

"Oh, I am sorry, Monique. I should have asked you before. I like to wait until my clients feel ready to talk about things but, of course, sex is always a difficult subject to bring up since it is so personal and intimate." I hope that my indirect comments give her the encouragement to continue.

Feeling more assured, Monique starts to warm to the subject. "Yeah. And it feels like I am betraying Sebastian by talking about it when he isn't here. Except that he is never here because he is always at work. Like Jacques and I are at the bottom of his list. Oh, I know you are going to tell me he doesn't really believe that, but you know it is still hard because of how he acts."

More assertive now, I say, "O.K. I am here for you and I want to know what is bothering you about sex. Sex is a special part of marriage. It should be about making love and a bonding time for a couple, not just sex. Is there a problem for the two of you?"

What's Wrong with an Agenda?

"Yes, there is," Monique announces emphatically, sounding more like her take-charge, outgoing self. Apparently my encouragement is working.

"Let me tell you what happened just last night," Monique continues. "I was getting frustrated with Sebastian because he never wants to make love any more. In fact, we really haven't made love since Jacques was born. Honestly! I know it is shocking. He says he loves me, but he is never in the mood. Maybe he's tired from all of the work he is doing. But it makes me feel unloved." Again she searches my face for approval. I am not shocked, and she senses that. I nod and give her a look that lets her know it's O.K. to continue.

"So any way, last night I asked Sebastian to leave the computer and come to bed with me. Is that such a bad thing?"

Monique launches into a dramatic replay of what happened the previous night.

"Now?" he said as if a wife asking her husband to bed is something strange and out of the ordinary.

His abrupt question made me burst into tears. "Sebastian, we have not made love in three years. What is wrong with you? Is it me?" Oh my God, he just kept staring at me as if I was nuts for asking these things. He has this way of staring at me when he is stumped. How on earth can a man be stumped about sex? Aren't men supposed to want sex more than women?

He finally blurted out a pitiful defense. "That's not true!" And then he turned to go back to his computer as if the discussion was over. He ignored my tears, my broken heart. Doesn't he need sex or at least a cuddle? What's wrong with this guy any way? Why can't he talk with his wife? And why do I have to bring up the subject of sex in the first place? I have to do everything in this relationship, and it just makes me crazy.

It is true. We haven't had sex in forever and it is so sad for me and so embarrassing to talk about. I got out of bed and walked over to the computer room and started screaming at him. "You idiot! How can you say it's not true? I might as well have the doctor take out the IUD . . . we never have sex any more. We were in bed with each other all of the time when we first met. You seemed so thrilled. That's how we got pregnant. But after the baby and our move out here and your new career and all of that stuff, you never touch me any more. You don't even look in my direction. And your kisses are like kissing a fish any way. There is no life in them. Are you having an affair?" I was mad and hurt and feeling crazy like I do whenever I try to reason with this man about the obvious. I feel badly that I lost my temper, but it is so unnerving.

Sebastian said, "What are you talking about? Can't you see I'm busy right now? You're being irrational. We can have sex when I come to bed later." Sebastian just says the most stupid things at times like this. I want him to understand my feelings. I want him to know how much I miss him. I want him to drop everything and hold me and tell me it will get better. I know I am being childish, but is it so wrong to want your husband to come to bed with you once in a while?

"Oh yeah! You're never too busy for work or the Internet, are you Sebastian?" I got sarcastic, as if that will work. The anger was rising in my body, and I felt my fists clenching. I wanted to hit him, to somehow get even for the pain he was causing me. When I felt how hot my face was getting, I knew I was getting out of control – and over what? Sex? It can't be so important that I destroy our relationship over it. So I stopped. I didn't want the baby to be upset. He's old enough now to understand these things and he always tries to protect Mommy. I don't want that. So I shut down for a minute or two and got a bit under control . . . Then I tried again.

"Sebastian, I'm sorry I was yelling at you. You don't deserve that. It's just so confusing to me. Other husbands look forward to coming home to their wives and making love. I know you think we do, but we don't. It really has been three years since we made love. Well . . . maybe we have had a time or two in there, but it wasn't love making. It was not sensuous. Most of the time I have to masturbate to reach a climax because you don't seem to understand what I need or take the time to really BE with me. I hate to sound like I am blaming you, but you don't

try. You don't listen. You just don't seem to understand what I need. Do you understand what I am talking about?"

The tears were streaming down my face as I implored Sebastian to listen and understand my distress. But he still seemed unmoved. I can never read his face. I guess emotions are so confusing to him that he just shuts down.

He stood there. He didn't walk away. Just stood there. No comment. No emotion. No argument. I think I could see the wheels turning in his head. He looked like Jack Nicholson in the movie Something's Gotta Give *with Diane Keaton when she is yelling at him and crying about what she needs. You know the movie, don't you? Nicholson just stands there dumbfounded, not knowing what to say or how to comfort her, like sex is just a commodity – not a living, breathing, incredibly important connection between lovers.*

"Sebastian! Please talk to me. Work this out with me. I am your wife. I just want you to come to bed with me. Say something!"

And then he did say something . . . slowly . . . and I don't have a clue why he would say something so weird. He looked at me like he was on another planet talking to an alien. He said, "Well, it is hard for me to come to bed with you because you always have an agenda." And then he went back to the computer, leaving me standing there speechless.

Monique's eyes were wide with amazement. "I was speechless, thoroughly speechless – and as you know, that is not easy for me. How do you respond to a stupid comment like that? An agenda? An agenda? Of course, I have an agenda. That's why I asked him to bed. But after hearing this ridiculous comment, I wasn't even hurt any more. I wasn't angry. I felt nothing at all. Stunned maybe. What do you think? Did I marry an idiot?"

Monique sat there looking just as stunned as she probably looked the night her husband accused her of having an agenda. What a crazy mixed message Sebastian had just delivered.

Is Sex a Commodity?

I remain calm in the face of Monique's dramatic monologue. She needs me to help her reason this out, even though she has a broken heart. "No Monique, of course, you didn't marry an idiot, but you did marry a man with Asperger Syndrome. I am so sorry that you have to go through this. I had no idea that your love life was so barren. But it is predictable. Many men with Asperger's have a hard time in this department. If you think about it, it makes sense. Aspies have trouble relating to the nonverbal communication in relationships, and sex is about as nonverbal as it gets. In fact, for sex to be real love making, partners need to pay exquisite attention to the nonverbal cues that each is giving."

"Please don't tell me he isn't going to get better!" Monique looked desperate. She has waited so long to get married again and have her one and only baby. She wanted so much for this marriage to work and to have love ever after.

I realize that just giving Monique the facts about Asperger Syndrome and sex is no help. That is just more of the "Mr. Spock" logic that makes her hurt and feeling lost.

"I don't know if he will get better at love making, but we have to take it one step at a time. First, since you are in my office and Sebastian is not, I have to work with you. I want you to become an expert in Asperger communication so that you can help him make some changes. But we can't force Sebastian to become the kind of lover you need. It's not always fair living with an Aspie, but there are answers."

Monique is not alone. Hers is a common problem. Many men with Asperger Syndrome start avoiding sex with their wives because they cannot seem to get it "right." Their wives expect the relationship to deepen over time. They expect the normal give-and-take in the bedroom that they expect in other aspects of the relationship. But if empathy and reciprocity is difficult in general for those with Asperger's, why would they be any better in the bedroom? In an environment that is ninety percent nonverbal?

Following a schedule. Being obsessive-compulsive. Having finite rules. These are the things that guide those with Asperger

Syndrome. But when it comes to relationships, especially love relationships, these approaches take the zest out of romance. That's why Monique exploded and accused her husband of "kissing like a fish." Sebastian had learned how to relate to Monique and was following the protocol he had learned when they were dating. He didn't adapt to a new type of kissing or a new touch with the nonverbal cues his wife was sending him . . . because he doesn't read those things. He has to be told, and then he has to incorporate the new information into his repertoire. Very complex and very different from the NT, who just lets it roll like Monique does.

Poor Sebastian. He did give Monique some genuine and helpful feedback if she could only listen to it. When he told her that she had an "agenda" whenever she asked him to bed, he was reading her nonverbal signals correctly. Of course, she had an agenda! She was hoping for sex or at least a few kisses and a little cuddling. There is nothing wrong with that. But Aspies can be stumped about how to deal with the NT's agenda, especially if they have disappointed their spouse over and over again.

Monique has been very critical of her husband's love making and communication in general, so it is only natural for Sebastian to avoid the situation after a while. When Sebastian mentioned that his wife had an agenda, what he needed to add was that her agenda made him nervous. She had no idea that her sexual needs made her husband nervous. That is the crux of the problem for many Aspies and NTs.

In fact, many NTs avoid sex for these very reasons. Even after years of communicating poorly about intimacy, romance and sex, NTs can be confused about resolving these marital problems, too. If this area is difficult for an NT (as evidenced by the hundreds of books and women's magazine articles on how to spice up your sex life), just imagine the struggles that someone with Asperger Syndrome will have.

Monique may want more sex with her husband, but she would be satisfied with less if it were a more meaningful interaction. When she shot him with the criticism that "your kisses are like kissing a fish," she was addressing a quality issue in the bedroom. While many Aspies are quite adept at studying human behavior and becoming masters at the many subtleties required to be convincing, such as many Hollywood actors, this doesn't mean they are addressing the here and now of a living, breathing, dynamic human interaction. After a while their lovers figure out that something is missing in their love making. Technique is not everything. Monique considered Sebastian's kisses were like kissing a fish because she felt his kisses were "cold," not filled with passion for her or an understanding of what she needed right now – at this moment in time.

This is an entirely different issue than the avoidance that often sets in when Aspies feel inadequate in the bedroom. Sensing that their lover is unsatisfied, even after they have done everything they know how to do and are unable to ask or gather guidance from the abundant nonverbal behavior their sweetheart is sending them, Aspies slowly pull away from these unpleasant encounters, leaving their partner even more frustrated. Avoidance compounds the already existing problem that the Aspies are not responding to the sensitive, in-the-moment requirements of their lover. This combination can lead to more than frustration over the relationship. It can lead both partners to believe they are unloved, and then the love starts to melt away.

The bottom line is this: Sex is not a commodity, but that is how many Aspies see it. So much of the problem they have relating to their NT loved ones stems from the fact that they are trying to figure out the rules, as if it is about moving chess pieces on a game board. In addition, most Aspies have developed rigid protective behaviors after years of being unable to regulate their overactive sensory systems.

Can you imagine how difficult it must be to have sensory overload and yet be expected to tune into your spouse's sensory needs? Monique named it correctly. Sex and love making are not commodities. They are processes that vary in the moment, depending upon the multiple interacting factors involved . . . factors such as timing, mood, energy level, need for variety and . . . sensuality. Very simply, NTs get this, and Aspies do not.

Solutions: No Sex, Affairs or Other Options

Most spouses have an inkling of an idea when their partner is having an affair. It's not the lack of sex in the bedroom that is an indication of an affair. Most Aspies do not have extramarital affairs because they are loath to break the rules. Plus, if they love their partner, there is no reason to seek another, even if sex has disappeared from the relationship, at least to their way of thinking.

However, the reverse is not as true. Many NT spouses seek out other partners to compensate for the lack of passion in their love life. Sex is either boring or non-existent in their marriages, but they still love their partner. And oddly, they often feel there are many things that still work well in the marriage even without sex. In fact, sex was probably not high on the list of reasons they chose their Aspie partner in the first place. All the same, when the sex falls away, these partners get desperate for the kind of affection and connection that comes with making love – and as a result seek it elsewhere.

Obviously, this creates a new set of problems. The NT feels guilty for his or her actions, but compelled nevertheless. The NT secretly hopes the affair will bolster the marriage somehow or that his or her partner will finally come around. But the opposite usually happens. Since the Aspie is not having conflicts with the NT spouse over sex any longer, he or she relaxes and forgoes sex altogether. The Aspie seems happily ignorant of the affair and settles into a sexless life.

I know of one NT wife who texts her boyfriend on her cell phone while she is in bed watching TV with her husband. The husband with Asperger's is clueless. Because he is watching TV and his wife seems content, and because he is not having an affair, it never crosses his mind that she would be texting a boyfriend.

So what's a couple like this to do? It always comes down to cooperation in treatment. If only one person is willing to work on a solution, you can only go so far. While Sebastian has acknowledged his Asperger Syndrome, he hasn't taken seriously the fact that he needs to be in psychotherapy or that he needs an education in sexual etiquette. His wife of only three years is about to explode and is very vulnerable to having an affair. Ideally, she will not go in that direction because of the obvious threat to trust in the relationship. But Monique can only do so much on her own. Without her husband's participation in treatment, they will have a rough go of it.

Ideally, the Asperger partner will let go of his trepidations. He will put himself into his wife's hands and allow her to lead their sexual encounters. Equally so, the NT needs to let go of the belief that the Aspie husband should do the wooing. He isn't cut out for it. Oh yes, he was very attentive at first . . . when she was a novelty. But after a while he cannot attend to her every need and nonverbal communication, and manage his own sensory overload at the same time. It is too much work and too much translating for him. But if you get the egos out of the way, things can work.

Be explicit. If you guide his every move, you may be able to restore some romance to your life. Aspies need to be prepared. They need to know what will happen next. Schedule romance. Schedule bedtime. Schedule the children for events so that you can have alone time with your spouse. The Aspie loves schedules and will adhere to them. Watch an erotic movie together and practice what you watched. You may lose the thrill of spontaneity, but that is a small price to pay for a more attentive lover who is ready for you because it is on his schedule and he is prepared to connect.

And don't forget to bring this issue up with your therapist. Sex and intimacy are high on the list of things that are problematic for all couples, not just NT-Asperger couples. Because this is such an emotional issue and often quite volatile, you might need the calm, objective outlook of your therapist to help you get perspective. Usually the sexual dysfunction is not physical but a mental block such as we have seen with Sebastian and Monique. Let your therapists help you devise a strategy to break through the misunderstandings.

Lessons Learned

1. Be brave and tell your therapist that you are having sexual problems in your marriage to an Aspie. Otherwise how can you move forward?
2. Stop being hurt by the lack of affection in your relationship. Your Aspie partner probably loves you but doesn't know how to show it. If you feel hurt, you remain a victim and helpless.
3. To resolve these problems, you have to do the same work with your partner as you do with other aspects of communication, and that means both of you have to be in therapy.
4. Because the Aspie is such a concrete thinker, the NT needs to take charge of sex and love making with a reluctant lover. Be direct, specific and concrete in your guidance of love making with your Aspie lover.
5. If your partner will not work with you, don't descend into unethical behavior such as having affairs. They wreak havoc in lives. But do make choices to reclaim your life. No one should have to live with love in the deep freeze.

CHAPTER SEVEN

Recognition

Miranda, another client, is making one last-ditch effort to save her marriage when she and her husband learn that Norman has Asperger Syndrome (AS). For them the diagnosis is a godsend.

In this chapter you will get a sense of hope for your marriage or relationship with a loved one with AS. While you can take back your life even if your Aspie loved one does not work with you, think of what you can accomplish if both parties take on the project of building an "interface protocol."

Freedom Begins with a Diagnosis

Marriage between a neurotypical (NT) and an Aspie can be tough, as you have seen in the preceding chapters. But there is one thing, above all else, that can ease the anguish and open the lines of communication. Probably the most important aid in breathing life back into the marriage is a diagnosis by a mental health professional . . . and coming to accept and use that diagnosis to refashion interpersonal understanding and communication.

While this may sound too clinical to some, the knowledge that you or your partner has Asperger Syndrome gives you both more to work with. Instead of stumbling around in the dark, and causing each other to feel like a loser, a diagnosis gives you a direction and a growing body of literature to read about the syndrome. This can be the true beginning of freedom. Let's see how this pans out for Norman and Miranda, who are both in my office for therapy.

No Expression on His Face

Norman sat very quietly; not a muscle moving, no expression on his face. He seemed to be listening, but I couldn't tell what he comprehended. I have seen this look before (the sliver in my mind) – not a hint of what is going on in his mind because there is no acknowledgment of what you are saying. No smile. No nod of understanding. Not even a sign of disagreement. Just listening and watching.

Cops and judges train themselves to look this way. They try to be neutral and impartial, without judgment. But even cops and judges give themselves away. The color changes in their faces. They squirm a bit. They look a little grimmer when they try to keep from conveying meaning. Norman's look is slightly different. It's just blank; like he is totally unaware that you are searching his face for meaning and connection.

Typical conversation is like a dance.

From the moment She looks at him, He recognizes that look. He moves from his seat and walks toward her. She raises her eyes to his and starts to stand up. Not a word is spoken before He reaches for her hand and helps her stand the rest of the way. "Would you like to dance?" She nods, takes his hand firmly and follows him to the dance floor. She smiles. He smiles. He touches her waist ever so slightly, and She moves in the direction of the pressure of his hand. She leans near him, and He drops his shoulder close to her cheek. She laughs softly and He breathes in the smell of her hair.

As illustrated in the previous paragraph, conversations, like a dance, are full of subtle expressions that convey thousands of unspoken words. To be sure, there are many misunderstandings as a result of "reading" the wrong meaning into a gesture or a blush, but even the very act of "reading" another person is a meaningful connection between people.

Such nonverbal subtleties are totally missing with Norman. He makes no attempt to offer these gestures, these nonverbal cues that send the message that he is with you, listening, comprehending – connecting with you. I look into his eyes and see nothing. I scan his face for some hint of recognition and again come up empty. *Unnerving, unsettling,* those are the words that describe the feelings his behavior evokes.

Norman doesn't give the dance partner a signal about what to do next. Yet, I do not sense that he is deliberately holding back. He is just unaware of my need for interpersonal feedback. I watch Miranda. She is easy to read. She is annoyed with Norman. She breathes a heavy sigh, rolls her eyes and turns toward me. She senses that I am connecting with her, so it is easier to talk with me than with Norman.

"I don't know why I bother. He's a good man, but he is always like *that*." She points in his direction. After three sessions with Norman and Miranda, I now understand what she means, but I ask the question anyway.

"What do you mean, 'always like that'?"

Exasperated, Miranda answers. "Oh God! I talk and talk and talk until I am blue in the face, and he just sits there, saying nothing. I cry, threaten and stir up a real storm, and still nothing! I might as well not try any more. Might as well get a divorce."

Norman moves, and we both turn toward him with excited anticipation. His voice holds a tense tone. "I'm tired of being criticized all the time. She never appreciates anything I do. I am trying to help, but I am told that I don't care enough. I am tired of being treated like a chump! I have feelings, too!"

There Is a Name for It

Norman and Miranda have been married for thirty-five years. They have three grown children, all of whom are college educated and in good careers. None of the children are married yet, even though they are in their late twenties and early thirties. But then they have been busy with college. Miranda, or Mandy as she prefers to be called, worries about them, though. She wonders why they have not found mates yet.

I think I know. The problems that plague Norman and Miranda and their family are eerily similar to those of Helen and Grant and their children. There is a pattern. After a complete psychological evaluation in my office, I unfold the pattern for Mandy and Norman.

"Norman, I bet you have had this experience with other people during your life time, maybe as a child, maybe even now at work. Do you know what I mean?"

Norman looks up at me with a sign of interest on his face. "You mean, people criticizing me and accusing me of not listening or not caring?"

"Yes," I reply. "And perhaps treating you as if you are not very smart or can't follow the conversation. At work, do people kind of ignore your suggestions? Or have you wondered why you are not promoted as often as others, even though you are just as smart? You know, maybe they have a bit more polish than you do."

I have his interest now and Miranda's as well. Miranda laughs. "Oh yes. That would be Norman!"

I continue. "Another way to look at this is that other people seem to know what is going on and you are a little out of step. It might even make you anxious that you can't follow the conversation as well as others, so you pull away."

"How did you know?" Norman is catching on. "I really have a hard time at meetings if there are more than one person talking. I just shut down and doodle instead. I am a manager, and I am supposed to track what is going on, but I cannot follow more than one person at a time. So I have to ask for a recap from someone after the meeting. They have to think I am brain dead. It is so embarrassing."

"You know, Norman, there is a name for what is going on here. I have been working with you two for a couple of weeks now, and I think I know what is complicating your progress. It is called Asperger Syndrome, or high-functioning autism." Mandy is all ears but looks astonished. She just thought her husband was a dud and a dullard.

"Asperger's is a developmental disorder, which means you were born this way and your brain grew differently than other people's. It has nothing to do with IQ. In fact, many people with Asperger Syndrome, or AS, are very bright and accomplished. But one of the most telling feature is the lack of interpersonal awareness and interpersonal skill."

Norman and Miranda are looking at each other now, then back at me. I can almost hear the computer chips humming in their brains as they process what I am telling them. Norman says, "That might explain what happened when I was a boy."

Miranda looks at him in astonishment. "What are you talking about?" She turns to me. "He never tells me anything about what went on in his past or what he feels about his life. He's like a robot. Now he has a past!?" Sarcastically she says, "Tell me more, Norm."

I immediately try to recoup the little emotional window of opportunity that Miranda nearly crushed. "Norman, look at me. I do want to know."

Norman looks at me and seems to have a look of trust (could be my imagination). "This may help us learn more about what is getting in the way for the two of you in your marriage. I know that Mandy is angry and has been for some time, but you need to know that anyone would be this way with the way you have handled things. If it is Asperger Syndrome, and both of you didn't know it, can you blame either one of you? Let's get to the bottom of things. So please tell me what you know about this from your childhood. I want to help."

Taking a breath, Norman carefully, methodically, and without a tear, tells his sad and painful story.

I had this experience when I was twelve. There was this girl at school who came up to me at recess and talked with me. She asked me for my phone number and wanted to know if she could call me. I was flattered and gave her my number. And she did call later. She acted real nice on the phone, telling me she liked me and all of that, but it ended there.

Later I learned that she was just making fun of me, because for weeks afterwards she would walk past my house with her girlfriends. They would point at the house or at me if I was out in the yard and laugh. She never said "Hi" or anything. She just pointed and laughed. I realize that I was the butt of some joke. You know, make fun of the shy kid type of thing. The truth is that I never really had any friends when I was younger, and most people don't go out of their way for me now either. I just don't fit in.

Miranda softens. "Oh, Norman. I had no idea. I'm just like those mean girls, I guess. I hate being this way with you, but I feel so lonely. I reach out to you and you just don't get it. So I get hurt and angry and want to hurt you back. I am so ashamed of myself."

Offering support, I intercede, "Mandy, don't beat up on yourself. Both of you are caught in the trap of not really understanding the problem you are facing. You have been coping the only way you knew how. But it has to change in order to get the love back in your lives."

"You know," I continue, "Norman's story from his childhood reminds me of a young woman with Asperger's. Childhood was very hard on her, just like Norman. And she still struggles with the rejection, though we are working on it in therapy. Even so, my heart breaks for her because she has the same kind of experiences that Norman described. She is shy, too. She likes to read and keep to herself. She feels safe in her books. And she loves to draw and listen to music. These things are her friends when she can't relate to people in real time."

"Me, too," says Norman. "I like photography, although I never seem to get anywhere with it."

"Well, we can work on that, too," I respond encouragingly. "It's hard to get anywhere with a hobby like that when you don't know how to share your love of photography with others. It is the pleasure that flows between people that makes the world go around. You will have trouble learning to create this kind of flow, but we can work on it a bit."

The fact that Norman can relate to the young woman is a good sign. He can see beyond his own experiences and connect with others. I am hopeful that Mandy too will see the connections and generalize to her husband. Knowing that others have similar concerns can be enlightening and healing.

I describe the nineteen-year-old. "This young woman is only nineteen, but she is discovering a whole new world for herself since she learned about Asperger Syndrome. For example, she tells me that she can't read faces and does not remember what people look like from meeting to meeting. And she gets so frustrated trying to chit-chat with people, like at those meetings you were talking about, Norm. She asks me 'Why don't people just say what they mean?' She wishes that she didn't have to explain things at all to others. She says, 'I wish people could just read my mind and understand and then we could stop.'"

Still without an expression on his face, but getting as animated as I have ever seen him get, Norman slowly leans forward and says, "I know just what she means. That is exactly how I feel. What am I supposed to do about this?"

Miranda is a puddle of emotions. She has been listening intently to the interchange, stunned by the things she is learning about her husband of thirty-five years. A professional woman, she cannot believe she never figured this out before. She wants to talk, but this time she is speechless. The words are not forming.

"Miranda . . . Norman . . . I want you to do some reading about AS and then we will talk some more. You need to learn about the syndrome first so that we can see how it works in your lives. AS is not like a broken leg or diabetes. It is a syndrome of multiple traits, and Norman does not have all of them. And of the traits he does have, he has some in a greater or lesser degree. So a diagnosis doesn't mean a simple solution.

The Rose, the Thistle and the Therapist

I now turn to Miranda.

"Miranda, I know that you fell in love with Norman because he was kind, attentive and very intelligent. He wasn't like the other guys you dated. He made you feel special. Now the specialness has worn off, and you feel as if you are living with a robot that has no feelings for you. But it is not true! Norman still loves you, but AS makes it hard for him to convey what is in his mind and heart. Because he can't read faces or body language well, and because he can't show you with his eyes or his gestures, a huge chunk of interpersonal communication is lost between the two of you."

I look at Miranda who is all ears by now and let her know that I understand the pain she has been through. "Mandy, I know that you have been holding your breath, waiting for Norman to come alive with you and share the pleasures of life, but instead you saw the years disappear and you getting older in the meantime. This lack of nonverbal connection that means so much to most of us feels like a rose trying to stay alive on the desert." Tears came to her eyes, as she was comforted with the knowledge that she was not one of those mean girls Norman had referred to; only lonely.

"But as much as you have longed for the type of bond between lovers that evolves over time from all of those small touches, glances and whispers that we expect between couples, Norman has been deprived, too. He has lived in a world of his own. As much as you have been the rose on an emotional desert, Norman has been the thistle, living on very little and learning to depend on no one but himself."

My mind wanders as Norman and Miranda talk with each other about these new revelations. Norman's childhood story triggers in me a memory of another child from many years ago, before I knew much about AS. I remember one day when she shared a poignant experience from elementary school. She seemed sad and stressed as she told me this story. She was nine at the time. As I look back, the telltale signs of AS were showing by then, but I did not know enough to make the diagnosis at the time. I only wish I had understood better. It grieves me that she had to suffer alone.

As usual she had gone to the playground after lunch with the other children. Even though she preferred to stay inside, the teachers always insisted she go outside for fresh air and exercise. They did not understand her pain. She took a book with her and sat down at the edge of the grass away from the other children, so that she could have some peace after all the hubbub of the lunchroom. But she was not to get that peace.

Shortly after she had sat down, a couple of girls came up to her and asked what she was doing. She explained about the book she was reading. She genuinely thought they wanted to know about the book and her opinions. But the children laughed at her and said she was stupid for reading at recess instead of playing with the rest of them. She became frightened by the taunts and got up to get away from the girls. But she was helpless to defend herself.

By then a few more children had joined in and they began circling this little girl, taunting her and laughing. She just froze in place and cried, which encouraged the children all the more. They began walking and then running around her in a circle, waving their arms in the air pretending to be birds, scaring her and mocking her. She was terrified but could not take any action to protect herself from the abuse.

Eventually, a duty aide came to her rescue and chased the others away. The child told me that the playground aide was kind and invited her to hang out with her for the rest of recess. Many a playground duty aid becomes the only friend for an AS child.

After Norman and Miranda left my office, I needed some time to pull myself together. It is odd how the clients the psychologist needs for her own personal growth show up in her office at just the right time. I wasn't able to help that little girl when she came to my office because I was not familiar with Asperger Syndrome. I was kind and compassionate. I tried to help with her anxieties and shyness, but in truth we got very little accomplished because I kept approaching her from the reality of an NT – and she could not connect to me.

I am surprised that I have hung onto that feeling of helplessness after all of these years. Perhaps it is partly my own co-dependency and partly my NT reactions to those unnerving Aspie traits, even coming from a child. Will Norman and this young woman ever understand the pain that their lack of recognition causes their loved ones? Will they ever know what it is like to connect, to really see the mind and heart of the other person? Will anyone ever come to know the thistle within each of them for its beauty and endurance?

I began thinking about Helen, too. It took me a while to comprehend that she was living with AS at two different levels. It made sense with her daughter, since Jasmine had so many core symptoms of childhood Asperger Syndrome, but I did not recognize the disorder in Grant until much later. He was so accomplished in life that I overlooked the telltale signs. Just like Norman, Grant also cannot fully connect in the nonverbal ways that mean so much to Helen. Both men are very accomplished in their careers, although probably not performing at the level of their intelligence. Both men are liked by coworkers and neighbors, yet neither has any meaningful relationships outside of their wives, and as these therapy notes reveal, their marital relationships are suffering, too.

Helen is a very brave woman to hang in with an AS husband and an AS child, caught in the middle. Too bad that Grant will not come to therapy with Helen. Perhaps he will some day. But for now, he tells her, "Dr. Marshack is your friend. I don't need any help. I'm fine. But you go, honey, if it helps you."

Helen may have to take back her life on her own and leave the marriage behind one day, but there is hope for Miranda and Norman because they are willing to work on the relationship together. They will have their struggles, but knowing that each of them cares and understands a bit more contributes a lot toward surviving the struggles. Norman may not recognize Miranda's signals. He may never know how to send nonverbal signals, but at least now each of them knows that there is far more to the other's experience than meets the eye.

Lessons Learned

1. There is hope for your relationship if both of you are willing to seek help.
2. The bullying experienced by many Aspies in their childhoods may be part of the reason why they hold back in relationships in adulthood. Be compassionate.
3. The other half of the reason why Aspies "hold back" is that they are not wired for empathy, so they miss many nonverbal cues.
4. Don't be offended if they miss your cues. Be explicit. Use words to explain your emotional state and your needs and wants. They may still think you are too emotional, but what the heck! That's an Aspie for you.

CHAPTER EIGHT

Rage

Too many years of co-dependency and self-blame led Helen to bust loose in a destructive way. Many who live with an Asperger mate fear this type of rage. Some tell me they feel they will simply die if they have to go on in the relationship.

In this chapter I hope you will begin to recognize the problem of denying your anger and keeping it pushed away. I will offer ways for you to know your anger and redirect that powerful energy before it turns to rage, and you feel pushed to the edge.

Emotionally Starved and Confused Without Reciprocity

Much has been written about the challenges of those with Asperger Syndrome (AS), but very little is understood about the destructiveness of living for years without emotional reciprocity. Neurotypicals (NTs) know their inner selves in relationship *with* others. Without that important emotional connecting that goes on every day in every human encounter, NTs can become so psychologically starved and confused that they are ready to explode . . . or implode. The experience is very much like insomnia. Chronic insomnia leads to more than fatigue. It can lead to psychotic-like episodes and a host of health problems.

Similarly, years of co-dependently covering for an AS family member, and with no one to turn to for the intimate connection of a sweetheart, the NT's coping mechanisms wear out. Self-destructiveness is not far behind in the form of over-eating, drinking abusively, having affairs – and unrelenting anger, sometimes leading to violence. Too few in the mental health field fully understand the anger that grows when your heart is broken day after day by the confusing behaviors of somebody with Asperger Syndrome. For example, after years of marital oppression, Helen's cool is finally shattered and her suppressed anger erupts.

Covering Up

I was curious about the cruise, but for the next ten days or so, I focused on other things while Helen, Grant and their children went on vacation. Nevertheless I kept coming back to that sliver in my mind. I ruminated on the way Helen covers for Grant. She does that for Jasmine, too. When Helen relates how Jasmine dominates the conversation with a monologue, chooses to eat in her room in front of the computer when the family has guests to dinner, or ignores Helen's entreaties to bathe and to shampoo her hair, I notice that Helen often makes excuses for her. She explains that Jasmine is very intelligent and artsy – kind of eccentric. She tells others that Jasmine is a teenager and "you know how temperamental they can be." To herself, Helen warns that she needs to be patient with her daughter and reassures herself that Jasmine will some day "come around."

That is a mother's love for you, and Helen will love and protect Jasmine forever. But something is odd about Helen protecting Grant. She lives a double life, maybe triple. She is the strong, assertive and kind professional woman. She is the loving, nurturing, and perhaps overprotective, mother. And she is the fatigued and emotionally oppressed wife.

Why does it bother me so that Helen covers for Grant? Lots of wives and husbands cover for their spouses or partners – both in healthy and in co-dependent ways. But I just froze in place when I witnessed the exchange between Helen and Grant in my office. Grant's oppressive behavior is subtle. I doubt that others notice it much. Just like Jasmine, he ignores the signals from others. He takes credit for ideas that are not his but that he has accepted as his own. He jokes with me in inappropriate ways. For example, he sports a big grin and chuckles as he says, "I can't imagine how you make so much money for what you do," but doesn't notice that I am not laughing. And how can Grant take credit for this vacation when he actively resisted it? How can he voice compassion for Helen and how hard she works, when he never lifts a hand to help her? How can he schmooze with me when he hardly knows me and seems to care little about Helen's therapy?

Of course, it could be a case of counter-transference – of the therapist seeing a bit too much of herself in her client. No doubt, that is a large part. I like Helen. I understand her heartache because we both have family members with AS. And Grant's behaviors are symptomatic of AS, too. Helen and I have speculated on this possibility. So perhaps I get annoyed with Grant because I know that tired feeling personally . . . tired of not being understood . . . tired of the constant caretaking that is required of NTs in a family of Aspies . . . tired of cutting off my life in service to my AS family members. When I hear of Grant's insensitivities to Helen, I suppose I overreact and take it personally.

Exotic Vacation for One

Once more Helen tells an enigmatic story about her life with Grant.

I watched with horror as Grant dragged his briefcase onto the plane for our trip to Mexico. He wasn't taking a few *papers but a catalog case stuffed with work to complete on our short vacation. As soon as we were seated on the plane, he pulled out his laptop and began to work.*

"Grant. We're on vacation. Do you suppose you could do that some other time? I mean, you know, this is exciting – a time to enjoy each other and the children." I tried to be supportive, but I was so disappointed that I wanted to cry.

"What do you mean? I always take work with me," he said. "I have important clients to consider here. You know that my boss expects this project completed or at least well under way by the time I get back. I had to twist some arms to get the boss to let me leave for this little boondoggle of yours. Besides, you can sleep and the kids can watch movies on their DVD players. What's the problem?"

Why do I bother? Grant has no concept that I would like some attention. Just a little love, a little communication, would mean so much. He is content burying himself in his work and leaving me to care for the twins. And the comment about the trip being a "boondoggle," that really hurt! Especially since Grant can't balance the checkbook. I manage our finances, because in his hands we would be bankrupt. But this trip isn't about money. It's about being a family and creating fond memories. Why can't he see that?

As you can imagine, the rest of the trip was not much better. Grant worked when I strolled the deck of the ship. Grant worked when I went to the bar and listened to music. Grant worked when I went to the pool with the children. Grant worked when I went into the towns along the way with the children to shop and tour. He did come with us on one excursion into the mountains. He hated the heat and the mosquitoes, and he was afraid to eat the food because of parasites, but he was willing to come along.

I was so grateful that the twins didn't fight. Jasmine was fascinated by the Mexican culture. She even let me buy her a Mexican party dress. She looked so pretty when we fixed her hair and she put on the dress for dinner that night, but then last minute she became afraid and refused to go to the dining room. Her anxieties got the best of her, and rather than risking a meltdown, I let her stay in the room for dinner. I am so disappointed when these things happen. I want so much for Jasmine to be normal and it almost happens . . . then something happens.

One Small Bit of Connection

Helen continues about the second leg of the trip.

Disneyland was a bit more fun. Grant stayed in the hotel room and worked while the kids and I explored the theme parks. There is something about Disneyland that allows Jasmine to relax and let go of her anxieties. She loves fantasy, so I think she ignores the crowds and enters the world of make-believe and takes us along with her. She has a gift of incredible imagination and storytelling. It was like having my little girl back again – before the Asperger's took over. The three of us giggled about silly things, and we screamed on the roller-coaster rides. We all really love the "Indiana Jones" ride. It's a hoot.

Jasmine was a great tour guide. She had read up on the theme parks before we went and was full of great tips on how to enjoy the parks to the fullest. Her favorite ride was "Soaring Over California." We went on that ride three times. We were almost like three kids on an adventure. In fact, Jasmine really took over at Disneyland. She was full of clever things to say, just like her dad when he is in a good mood.

Here's one for you. We were walking along in "California Adventure" by the Grizzly Bear Rapids, along a stretch of pavement made to look like the old Route 66, with worn yellow stripes down the center of the road. We noticed a mom struggling with her three-year-old, who had thrown himself on the pavement. He was screaming and wiggling all over the road, apparently a bit tuckered out by the excitement of the park. The mom was trying to control her child, but it was no use. Jasmine got that cute little smirk on her face, like when she is about to tell a funny one. She slowly and dramatically looked at me and at her brother and, with her dry sense of humor, she pointed at the child and said, "Road kill." Jason and I about bust a gut laughing. I felt the laughter pour out of me from deep down inside. It felt so good. For the rest of the day, all Jasmine had to do was point to another acting-out child, and we would all three say in unison, "Road kill," and start laughing all over again. Can you imagine?!

I don't think either of the children missed Grant at all. He did join us for dinner, but he wasn't particularly interested in hearing about our adventures at the park. He just wanted to make sure there was steak on the menu. That's Grant. He's a meat-and-potatoes man. No variety.

Helen had a few tears in her eyes as she talked about her daughter. I know that she wants to connect with Jasmine in the worst way. And what a wonderful healing experience for her to feel that joyful laughter from deep down inside and to be able to share it with Jasmine and Jason. If only every day with Jasmine could be at Disneyland.

I also noticed something different in her tone as she described Grant. She was more detached. What was that about?

Coming out from Behind the Marble

Helen concludes the story of the family vacation.

Flying home with Grant wasn't much better. Grant and Jasmine were nervous wrecks on the plane, worried about terrorists and losing our luggage. They both dither obsessively about everything. At one point I thought I had lost our passports, and both of them came unglued. They screamed at me that I could not be trusted and that we would all be arrested. Good grief. All I did was stuff the passports in the wrong pocket and had to search for a few minutes to find them. But they made it almost impossible for me to do that because I became so upset by their accusations. When I finally found the passports, they were both so upset that they blamed me for upsetting them, too. But we got home in one piece, with all of our luggage and our passports – and my sanity.

Turning toward me and away from her vacation story, Helen says, "I'm pretty convinced that Grant has Asperger's, too. I mean, he and Jasmine are so much alike. I could really see it on this trip. They both are crippled by anxiety and use all kinds of excuses to avoid anything new that frightens them. Grant's verbal abuse seems to have grown worse as the twins have gotten older. I have to soothe him as much as Jasmine in order to keep peace in the family. I have been thinking that it is time to get a divorce. This trip really brought home to me that I have no life with Grant. I have my work and the kids, but Grant is like an albatross around my neck. What's the point?"

You could have knocked me over with a feather. I had no idea that this would be Helen's next move. I have been through so much with her that I expected her to continue adapting to Grant. But she seemed serious. We talked for a bit about why she had this change of heart and if she had a plan. She didn't have a plan yet, but she said she wanted to talk more about it at our next session. Our time was up, so we had to table the discussion.

So that was the reason for the detached tone earlier, I thought – she was already signaling that she had let go of Grant.

One thing I have learned in my years as a psychologist is that many women do not give up easily when it comes to their marriages, especially the intelligent, nurturing and overly committed types like Helen. But once they do decide, there is no going back. When they are done, they are done! This seemed to be the case for Helen. The denial was over. The shields were dropped. The defenses melted. Helen was coming out from behind that translucent marble wall and warming up. I hoped I could help her through the process, especially because of her children and their need for safety at this stage of their lives. Divorces can get dicey, especially after years of marital distress.

Unleashed Rage

My cell phone beeped, alerting me that I had a call. I was working late at my desk, skipping dinner to finish up a report that was due the following morning. After taking a moment to print it out and put it in my secretary's box, I called my voice mail to pick up the message. There were actually two calls, one from Helen and one from her son, Jason. Helen's voice was strong with a sense of urgency.

Kathy, it's awful. I need your help. Grant kicked Jasmine again, and I got so furious that I slapped Grant in the face. I hit him so hard that I knocked his glasses off his face. I got so angry with Grant for his abuse that when I saw his glasses flying across the room, I stomped on them and crushed them, too. It was like slow motion. I couldn't believe it was happening. Jasmine's hiding in her room petrified to come out, but Jason got scared and called the police. Please, please call me back. I am worried. Am I going crazy? I can't believe I hit Grant.

When I heard Jason's message, my blood went cold. He sounded terrified. Who was there for Jason?

Dr. Marshack, this is Jason. The police arrested my mom. I didn't mean to do it. I called the police because Mom and Dad were fighting. Dad kicked Jasmine again. I tried to stop him, but he punched me in the ribs. Mom hit Dad, too. I wanted them to stop. I wanted the police to help. Dad is so upset right now. Jasmine is crying. Please call me back. I don't know what to do.

When I hurriedly called back, Grant answered the phone. He sounded fairly calm and said that he had things under control. However, he asked if I could call Helen and make sure she was all right. He also asked me for the name of an attorney to help her. Grant acknowledged that they had been fighting over disciplining Jason and Jasmine and that it had gotten out of control. He told me that Helen hit him and that this was not the first time. For a long time he had been worrying about her temper outbursts. "She seems to just erupt out of the blue! The kids are a big part of the problem. Helen will not let me discipline them at all."

My heart sank when I heard the story. Clearly, Helen was ready to leave the marriage and had no illusions any more that Grant could be her partner. She was also no longer able to bear the burden of covering for Grant when he abused the children. Unfortunately, she did not comprehend the anger that was stored up inside her after years of mind-numbing psychological oppression. Yes, Helen had decided to leave the marriage, but had she waited too long?

Lessons Learned

1. Don't let fatigue overturn your common sense. You need breaks, long breaks from your Aspie loved ones in order to be able to handle the responsibilities and challenges of these relationships, or you will explode.
2. Anger is a signal, a healthy signal, telling you that something is wrong in your life. But repressed anger makes you sick. When you have unresolved anger, you are more likely to make poor judgments.
3. When you stagnate in co-dependency, everyone suffers. Break this pattern. Get professional help and go to support groups.
4. By the time you consider divorce, you may already be "over the edge." Resolving the kinds of problems that cause domestic violence requires intensive psychotherapy for all family members.
5. If your partner will not seek therapy with you, it is important that you consider divorce as an option before the situation leads to violence.

CHAPTER NINE

The Sliver Comes Loose

While Helen may still be worrying about that sliver in her mind, the sliver is finally freed in my mind when I recognize my own mother's Asperger (AS) tendencies. When neurotypical (NT) children grow up with an Aspie parent, they are being defined by someone with a different "operating system." This can lead to a faulty and confusing sense of self.

In this chapter you will learn to take back your sense of self, regardless of how others see you.

Can You Be NT in an Aspie World?

We know very little about what happens when children with AS grow up and marry. And we know even less about what happens for children who grow up with Asperger parents. Some of the children with Aspie parents have Asperger's, too, but many are NT.

How do these NT children come to know themselves when reared by one or two parents who lack empathy? How do they develop a sense of self-esteem when their identity is not mirrored by their Aspie parent? How do they develop healthy relationships with others when their parent role models struggle with relating themselves? Fortunately, human beings are lifelong learners and can transcend childhood *mishigas* (a Yiddish word for *craziness*).

"It Just Snapped"

I have heard these stories from people who are married to a spouse with AS. They tell me that they lose control and become what they hate. They yell at their partners, berate them and become cynical and sarcastic – much like Mandy did with Norman. In Helen's case, years of making no headway in her marriage, feeling disconnected and lonely, and crazy for feeling this way, tied to protecting her children from their father's abusive outbursts, led her to fall apart. She couldn't take being "beaten up" any more and turned into the abuser.

It's classic co-dependency, such as you often see in alcoholic homes. Instead of detaching earlier and accepting that she could not change Grant, Helen kept trying and failing, trying and failing, trying and failing. Worn down emotionally and cut off from her true nature for so long, she snapped, and the marriage veered perilously toward a love-hate relationship. Like George and Martha in Edward Albee's play *Who's Afraid of Virginian Woolf?* after twenty years of marriage, it just snapped.

There was little I could do for Helen until she was released from the county jail. Fortunately, she did not have to spend the night in jail. I gave Grant the name of a good attorney, who helped him post bail and bring Helen home. We talked briefly over the phone when she got home, but Helen was so exhausted and demoralized that all she wanted to do was shower and go to bed. I told her that I would make the time for her, that she did not have to wait until her next appointment.

But I didn't see Helen until two days later. She is that kind of person. It is hard for her to believe that anyone would be there for her even at a time like this. But I respected this choice and waited for her to call.

Helen's skirmish with Grant wiggled my sliver loose a bit more. I have had to help clients with many crises such as this one. It is the sadder part of my work, but these events can also be a breakthrough in therapy. Pushed to the point of snapping and behaving out of character, and in such a destructive ways, is a wakeup call that few can ignore. But it wasn't just Helen's wakeup call. Once again, Helen's life was pushing me to examine my own.

My Mother, Asperger's and Me

Sometimes I can read several pages in a book before it occurs to me that my conscious mind has processed nothing. I always thought it was due to all those years of programming from two-dimensional teachers who insisted that you read a certain number of pages, instead of reading to learn. Then later, as a thirty-something adult, when I was diagnosed with dyslexia, I attributed my "spacing out" to the fact that it got too hard to read after a while. Still later, in mid-life, while working on my Ph.D., I was told that my "spacing out," or boredom, could be repression. In other words, something important could be happening on those pages that I could not or would not "see."

I picked up my book to read, found where I had left off the night before and commenced my evening reading mid-chapter. Soon it was clear to me that I was reading gibberish, so I dutifully went to the beginning of the chapter to start from the top. I really wanted to "grok" everything in this book, edited by Karen Rodman,[2] of collected essays and poems from partners, parents and family members of adults with Asperger Syndrome.

My ongoing research on Asperger Syndrome had led me to this book written by people who knew what it was like to live this life. It wasn't a clinical book or research, but the stories of real people. I was thinking a lot about Helen. A chapter by Judy Singer, "When Cassandra Was Very, Very Young," was about growing up with an AS mom. I knew that I would find gems in this chapter that might help Helen's son Jason and ease Helen's mind as well. She worries so much about Jason's emotional conflicts with his sister and his father. And she worries about how all of this conflict will affect his future relationships.

---

[2]Rodman, K. (Ed.). (2003). *Asperger's Syndrome and Adults . . . Is Anyone Listening?* London, UK: Jessica Kingsley Publisher.

Reading about Judy's mom got me to thinking about my own mother. My mom was a bundle of contradictions. In the past, my stories of childhood were a novelty to friends, who were alternately amused and horrified by what I would tell them. Like the time Mom got a good deal on shoes at a store closeout. Unfortunately, my new school shoes in eighth grade were bowling shoes! Embarrassing. Or the time that Mom left her keys in the car and went into a restaurant for lunch, only to return to her car an hour and a half later to find it still running and locked.

But there were more painful moments, such as the time Mom thought I was careless in my hygiene as a young teen because I was starting to get acne (what teen doesn't?). She decided to wash my face for me and scrubbed it so hard that my skin was raw for a week. And when Mom was really angry, she could "cuss a blue streak." My sister and I never knew when she would explode. In fact, Dad recognized early on that Mom could be abusive (such as the time she threw a cast iron skillet at my sister and narrowly missed her head), so wisely they agreed that she could not discipline the children.

I mostly remember my chain-smoking mother as depressed and sullen, staying up into the wee hours of the morning, smoking and reading her magazines. I guess at that time of night she could find some peace from the hustle and bustle of civilization, and her own noisy brain.

So as I read Judy's chapter over and over to clear the fog and to open my consciousness to a new reality, I realized I was reading this chapter for me, not for Helen. It dawned on me (actually, it hit me like a thunderbolt) that my mother probably had Asperger Syndrome. That would explain the eccentricities, the perceptual distortions, the lack of maternal empathy, her brilliance and her social ineptitude. It would explain why so many of her conclusions made no sense to me, even as a child. It might explain why she had a "nervous breakdown" when I was fourteen and was shipped off to the local state mental hospital for shock treatments. But more important, it would come to explain my own confused self-perception. How could I get to know myself if I kept looking into the mirror of my mother's world and getting no reflection?

Mom's Struggle with Death

One of my last memories of Mom was her death. It is a strange memory of grief unresolved that carries forward to this day, over thirty years later. It was grief for a woman who never knew me or *seemed* to care who I was. When Mom died at age forty-nine, I was tremendously relieved to be out from under the spell of confusion she had cast in my life, but I never knew what the problem was until I read Judy Singer's chapter. Only then did the sliver in my mind loosen and come free. As I read, memories from 1976 – the year my mother died – flooded over me.

I was twenty-five. I walked quietly into Mom's room at my aunt's house. I didn't want to disturb her sleep, but I wanted to be with her. I wanted to touch her, to share my love with her. Mom was dying from cancer, and there was little time left. She had decided to forgo treatment and to die at home, or at least as close to home as she could get, under the watchful eye of her sister-in-law and brother. I always thought it a brave move on Mom's part that she did not want to go through chemotherapy and radiation treatments. But I am not sure it was brave. She just didn't want the inconvenience if it meant six more months of painful living. Practical. Is that an AS trait?

I watched Mom sleep, but I secretly hoped she would wake up and talk with me one more time before there would be no other talks. I sat on the edge of her bed, gently took her pale hand in mine. It was moist and hot. Her body was working very hard against the cancer. It would not be long before it would overtake her. I watched her labored breathing. I could smell the decay. Her face was tense. This was not a peaceful sleep.

I noticed that someone had placed my candle on the TV set in the corner of the bedroom. A recent graduate of social work school with a master's degree, I could not think of what to do to help my mother in her struggle with death. So in desperation I had bought a candle with an inspirational message about "Faith" glued under a layer of white wax. Someone had placed the candle in direct view of my mother. I hoped she appreciated the gesture.

Mom awoke while I sat on the bed, moaned quietly and looked at me with great pain on her face. "I'm sorry, Mom. Did I disturb you?"

"Yes. It hurts," she responded.

"Oh, I am so sorry. Does it hurt when I sit on the bed?"

She nodded, so I reluctantly moved over to a chair. But then I could not touch her and feel her close to my body. I wanted to feel her live body next to mine, an attempt to feel some connection. But it caused her pain, and I couldn't bear that either. So I moved away and waited patiently for her to be with me once again.

Quietly and without opening her eyes, Mom spoke. "You could have done something about my pain." Mom was talking to me in that faraway manner that was the result of morphine and cancer and in that familiar monotone, emotionless voice I had heard so often during my childhood.

"What?" I had heard her very clearly, but thought she was confused about something. After all she was dying, and under the influence of morphine. My mother was a chain smoker. She even rolled her own cigarettes. She had lung cancer due to her addiction. So I was having a hard time understanding how I could have prevented this pain.

"You could do something so that I don't have to suffer like this," Mom said without looking at me.

I could feel the heat rising in my neck and face as I recognized the all-too-familiar manipulation that my mother had used on me over the years. She was making me responsible for her suffering, just as she had accused me of harming her so many times during my childhood. She used to tell me that I used too much hot water when I washed the dishes or that I didn't use enough soap. If I folded the towels, side to side, instead of end to end, I not only had to fold them over again, I also had to listen to her berate me for doing them wrong on purpose. One of her favorite expressions was that I did these things, "Just to spite her." It made no sense to me as a child that I was out to get my mother, but that is how she saw it. So here it was again, even near death, I had to endure my mother's irrational accusations.

"Do you mean that I could put an end to your suffering?" I asked incredulously.

"Yes," she said.

"Do you mean that I should poison you or something to end all of this?" another incredulous question escaped me.

"Yes," she said.

By now I was so agitated I couldn't see straight. I felt trapped. She was only forty-eight years old and struggling terribly with the disease. I hated to see her suffer, but I couldn't live with myself if I killed her. I wanted to help her through this last period of her life, but did I have to give up me to be there for her? Again? Was our relationship nothing more than a horrible game of blame, even to the end?

I was alone in the room. No one to hear this exchange. No one to ask for help. No one to comfort me. I couldn't stand feeling crazy. So I ran. I jumped up out of my chair and ran out of the room . . . but not before screaming at her, "That's not my job!"

A few weeks later Mom died, just a couple of days after her forty-ninth birthday. Dad was with her when she slipped into a coma. It was nighttime, and he was lying beside her in the bed. Her last words were to my father, as it should be. She must have had some kind of recognition that she was leaving, but all she said was "*Paul!*" and then she was gone. It has taken me another thirty years to recognize that Mom probably had Asperger Syndrome. With that realization, the above exchange takes on a new meaning.

Mom's Struggle with Life

I have a new appreciation for my mother's attempts to understand her world after learning that she probably had undiagnosed Asperger Syndrome. I can forgive her verbal abuse and her inadvertent denial of my reality. After decades of being rejected, no wonder she devolved into her own paranoid world.

She told me of life growing up on the North Dakota prairie in the Great Depression. My grandparents were German immigrants and homesteaders. When little Irene (my mother) was only two, her mother died, and she grew up with her gruff, intolerant father and four older brothers on a farm that never made any money. They were "dirt" poor. She slept on a mattress stuffed with cornhusks. She bleached flower sacks to make clothing. She had to cook for her dad and brothers over a wood stove. Once in a while she was allowed a treat of lard smeared on a piece of bread and sprinkled with sugar.

But she did have a few pleasures; solitary pleasures. One was to ride the plow horses bareback across the prairie, with her long black hair blowing in the wind. She told me she could feel happy and free on those days. Another pleasure she would take with her for the rest of her life was her joy of reading. It was through books that Irene learned the English language, since only German was spoken at home. And it was through books that Irene escaped the oppression of her childhood and dreamed about one day having another life.

I felt sad for my mom when she told me about the harsh life of growing up on the prairie. I heard all of those stories about poverty and walking miles in waist-high snow to get to the one-room schoolhouse, and in the case of my mother's childhood, these things were true. She also told me about being ridiculed and ostracized by the other children because she did not speak English when she started school at age six. I have always marveled at my mother's perfectly pronounced, grammatically correct English. She told me that she learned English by reading, since neither her teacher nor her classmates knew German – her native language – and wouldn't help her. It seemed so lonely to be that little girl. But I was proud of her for being smart enough to learn so much from books.

She was spunky, too. One time the other children would not allow her to play ball with them. So at an opportune moment, she stole the ball and hid it in a furrow in a neighboring farmer's field. Of course, the ball was lost to everyone when the farmer plowed it under, but my mother got even!

After reading Judy's chapter in Rodman's book, I had to rethink these stories about my mother. With the sliver freed, I could see the contradictions. I even laugh at myself for being drawn into her Asperger reality and accepting her analysis. Think about it. My mom grew up in North Dakota with a largely German immigrant population, at a time when German was probably spoken more than English. Those other kids at the one-room schoolhouse had German immigrant parents, too. They were all in the same boat. In fact, even today 43.9 percent of North Dakotans are of German ancestry, with Norwegians following at 30.1 percent. Good grief, the capital of North Dakota is Bismarck. You can't get much more German than that. Why on earth would my mother be convinced that no one spoke *her* language when she was growing up in German North Dakota in the 1930s – unless she was referring to the unique language and culture of Asperger Syndrome?

So if Mom was wrong about North Dakota, I had to seriously rethink my own notions of reality and my identity, especially those portions that were derived and deduced from Mom's reasoning. All of us have to grow up and come to know ourselves independently of others' opinions, but when your mother has Asperger Syndrome, there is an additional dimension to clear up.

Mom Taught Me to Be Brave

This is not to say that Mom was wrong about everything. Mom was eccentric. She liked to call herself "Bohemian." She wore sandals all year long, even in the snow, because it was more comfortable for her bunions. When other mothers wore shirtwaist dresses and aprons, my Mom wore jeans and my Dad's castoff Oxford cloth dress shirts, with the collars removed. She was a voracious reader. She would drag me to used bookstores and libraries to stock up on reading material.

Mom was a country girl from the North Dakota prairie and even though we lived in a suburb, she claimed you couldn't take the country out of the girl. We had a compost pile in the backyard, even in the 1950s. Mom made all our meals from "scratch." There wasn't a teaspoon of sugar in the house for years because Mom said it would "rot your teeth." And like a dog, my mother had a sixth sense about strangers. She could sniff out good people from bad as well as any hound dog. As a child I thought my mother was repressive. Later as an adult I came to think of her as being ahead of her time.

After Mom died, I had dreams about her. I still do. The dreams are always odd. Mom is walking around, but no one can see her, except me. I try to talk with her in these dreams, but she does not respond. It was no different in real life. I never understood why she was so tortured, but I accepted that it was so and kept my distance.

It is odd being so important to my mother. I was so important that she deemed it my responsibility to ease her suffering throughout her life and to her death. I was her "go-between" for the Asperger and NT worlds. But I made more meaning of her Asperger's thinking than she intended. She was just stating some facts when she asked me to poison her. She was suffering. She assumed that with my education I must know how to help her with her pain. And she asked me for help.

She wasn't thinking about the suffering this would cause me. She hadn't planned ahead either. But then who does plan ahead for death? I read about those brave people who receive the diagnosis of Alzheimer's and then call Dr. Kevorkian. I am amazed they can do it. Mom was not brave. She was simple. She just wanted a break. I was too young at the time to know this.

But there is an interesting paradox. By assuming a high level of importance to my mother, I became a hero. Mom taught me to be brave. I never felt loved by my mother, but I did feel important. That gave me a certain degree of confidence that others don't have. My ex-husband used to say, "Kathy, you go where angels fear to tread." I suppose this is true. I am willing to do what I think is right, even if others do not approve. I have a certain degree of empathy for the underdog. In spite of my mother's weirdness, I learned from her to be true to myself and not hold back in favor of fitting in. You will find in general that this is true of many children raised by Asperger parents. Even if we are NT, we are an odd lot.

Lessons Learned

1. Anyone can snap. If you do, immediately work through the crisis with your therapist. There are lessons to be learned.
2. Is there Asperger's in your family tree? Many NTs marry an Aspie because this is what they know from childhood.
3. Don't expect to find yourself in other persons, especially not Aspies, who can only reflect back to you what they know – not who you are.
4. Even at the most painful moments, try to detach and see the "Asperger Moment" for what it is – a statement of fact, not emotion.
5. Aspies can be quite defensive and suspicious after years of being bullied and misunderstood – and misunderstanding others.
6. Focus on the qualities you admire in your Asperger's loved one. They can teach you things that you would never learn otherwise.
7. Don't feel sorry for yourself or your children for growing up with an Aspie parent. You and your children may gain strength and wisdom from this experience.

CHAPTER TEN

Women and Asperger Syndrome

Asperger Syndrome (AS) has been described by some as "extreme male thinking."[3] If that is so, consider how difficult it can be to be female with AS. Barry and Katrina are a couple who both have Asperger's. Through their eyes you will see how trying it can be to communicate when two people have mind blindness and other traits of Asperger Syndrome and are raising children together as well.

Women with AS Don't Fit In

It is a harsh fact that women are valued for who they are, whereas men are valued for what they do. While we may joke about the eccentricities of men with AS, such as the stereotype of the absent-minded professor or the geeky software engineer, there are no similar acceptable and endearing stereotypes for women with AS. This is because women – all women, whether they have careers or work in the home – are valued for how well they fit in. Most women are well aware that they need to be pleasant, supportive and caring, or else leave themselves open to less complimentary labels.

---

[3]Baron-Cohen, S. (2004). *The Essential Difference. Male and Female Brains and the Truth About Autism.* New York: Basic Books.

For the woman with Asperger Syndrome, this gender imperative can be a nightmare. Fitting in is almost the antithesis of AS. How can you fit in when you don't have "social radar"?

Katrina is an example of a woman with AS who struggles with fitting in, even though she has crafted a successful career for herself. Married to Barry, a man with AS, Katrina not only has to manage her husband's idiosyncrasies, she also has to try to measure up to his notions of the ideal woman . . . all the while struggling with her own AS traits such as mind blindness, sensory overload and heightened anxiety. No wonder women with Asperger's can become suicidally depressed.

Parenting with a "Spousal Unit"

"What am I to do with my Spousal Unit[4]?" Barry looks at me seriously. "Katrina just barrels ahead with her plans and ignores all of us. I feel like an unneeded appendage in our household. For example, this weekend Katrina and the kids were arguing about something, and when I tried to help out, she accused me of interfering. She was screaming and crying, and so were the kids. When I told the kids, in no uncertain terms, to stop and go to their rooms, they minded me immediately. But then Katrina accused me of being too harsh, being a bully and undermining her authority. I get so depressed because we just don't have a relationship any more."

Barry has brought these concerns to me many times. He and Katrina both have Asperger Syndrome, as do their two children, Angelina and Albert. All are very bright and academically successful. Barry and Katrina have professional jobs and are financially well off. Their talents are well rewarded in the professional world but at home, with the chaos of raising children and managing a busy, creative household, Barry and Katrina are not the best of team players. Katrina tries to mastermind everything and demands that the entire family do as she tells them to do. Barry hangs back, much like one of the children, hoping for a little crumb of affection from his wife, but she is too busy masterminding to respond to his needs.

---

[4] The term "Spousal Unit" comes from the Coneheads script on *Saturday Night Live*. I have never heard NTs use this term to describe their partner, but apparently the quirky, sci-fi Conehead style appeals to many Aspies.

I console Barry. "Barry, you know that Katrina loves you, but she has a hard time accepting that she is not cut out for the Earth Mother Award." This is so true. Katrina reads every book she can find on raising children and managing a home. She attends seminars and support groups and reads the latest Internet research on raising happy, healthy children. Then she applies what she learns in a rather haphazard fashion, an inconsistency that wouldn't work with most children, let alone her brilliant children with Asperger Syndrome. She gets frustrated that her wonderful plans don't work out and then blames Barry for being unsupportive.

Barry continues. "Honestly, Dr. Marshack, I'm not sure I believe you any more that Katrina loves me. She sleeps with the children every night. She tells me that she has to so that they will fall asleep because they have such weird sleep habits. The kids get up in the middle of the night and play music or get on the computer. She tucks them in, crawls into bed with them and falls asleep there, and never comes to bed with me. Sometimes the kids get up anyway and are causing all kinds of commotion in the middle of the night, and their mother is sound asleep through it all – in one of their beds! I often have to take a nap after work, since I am so fatigued after a full day, but Katrina doesn't seem to care. She just wants to make sure the kids get to bed, but it isn't working."

Sleep problems are common for those with AS. Just imagine how difficult it must be to have this kind of problem and at the same time be raising children with sleep disorders. Barry is at a loss to get some time with his wife, deal with his sleep disorder and help his children, so he leaves it all to Katrina. Katrina feels the burden and does her best, but is spinning her wheels and getting more and more anxious.

Raising Children Is an Art, Not a Recipe

I have frequently talked with Katrina about their problems, too. Her story always sounds very different than Barry's. Like many women with AS, Katrina appears to be more sensitive to what it takes to organize the family. While Barry works, eats, sleeps, plays and loves his family, he has no awareness of the developmental needs of his children.

Somehow, in his view, the kids will grow up on their own, like seedlings in a forest. But Katrina knows that is not the case and wants desperately to meet their needs. The problem is that she is clueless about what these needs are, in spite of all her reading, classes and psychotherapy. In addition, as the children grow older and their Aspie ways become more apparent at school and in the neighborhood, Katrina has even more challenges to contend with.

Katrina shares her side of the story with me. "I suppose that Barry already told you about our little battle this weekend. He really knows how to crush Angelina's spirit. I was handling things just fine when Barry burst into the room and told Angelina to 'shut up' and go to her room or she would be spanked. I was sitting there quietly explaining things to her, trying to help her calm down from her tantrum. Well, yes, I was frustrated and crying, but I think Angelina was starting to listen to me. She was still kicking the cupboard door, crying and demanding that I give her ice cream before bedtime, but I believe it is important to remain calm and reasonable. Then Barry does his number, and it all falls apart."

These are the kinds of situations all parents have to negotiate. Most dads are a bit more adamant about obedience than moms. Most moms seem to think a reasoned approach will quell a tantrum. I suppose there is room for both approaches, depending on the circumstances. But when I try to explain the obvious to Barry and Katrina, they look stumped.

"Katrina, this is pretty normal behavior for a dad. It doesn't mean Barry is undermining you. He thinks he is helping. And after all, Angelina did stop her tantrum. I know that you wanted Angelina to be responsible for her own behavior, but sometimes when emotions are that out of control, you just have to break the pattern. That's what Barry did. Maybe it wasn't diplomatic, but it worked."

Katrina is frustrated with my interpretation. "But he wasn't helping at all. Angelina was crushed. I am following a plan, and if I wanted his help I would have asked for it." Katrina is assuming that Angelina was crushed. It could also be that she was relieved to have an end to a problem she couldn't work herself out of. All that Katrina knows is that she read an approach in a book and was going to use it for hours if need be, even when there was no evidence that it was working.

It takes a lot of work to help Katrina understand that raising children is an art, not a recipe. It is hard to get across to Aspies that most relationships are in constant flux and that the "right" answers "just depend" on the moment.

In another situation requiring the flexibility that so many Aspies lack, Katrina felt guilty for leaving her children alone in the afternoon after school before she and Barry get home from work. The kids are middle-school age and capable of fending for themselves for a couple of hours. I doubt that they minded the freedom and am certain that they didn't feel abandoned.

Even though I explained this repeatedly to Katrina, she insisted on worrying about it and decided to have a long heart-to-heart talk with the kids. When she asked them if they felt scared or abandoned, they both looked at her like she had two heads. Albert said, "I don't mind," and went back to his computer. Angelina at least thanked her mom for asking and then wanted to know if she could use her mother's cell phone to make a long-distance call. The next time I saw Katrina, she relayed all of this but still needed reassurance, asking me if it sounded like the kids were O.K.!

Clutter as a Way of Life

Katrina approaches household management no differently than she handles her parenting duties. She hunts for formulas, applies them haphazardly, fails, gets discouraged and then hunts for new formulas. Barry reports that their house is like a gerbil cage. There are boxes and piles of stuff stacked everywhere in every room. You can't see the kitchen table because of clutter. There are trails between the clutter barely wide enough to negotiate to get from one room to another. Katrina complains that the mess is due to lack of help from her husband, who comes home from work and sleeps until dinnertime. But how did the mess get this far out of control? It must be that no one in the house can comprehend how to organize for living.

To her credit, Katrina makes more of an effort than Barry. She has hired nannies and housekeepers, and even professional "organizers." Things go O.K. for a while, but then it all falls apart again. Life is a process that keeps evolving, and this is as true for a family household as it is for any other aspect of life. But the Asperger mind cannot grasp this concept. The rolling nature of maintaining a household escapes it. My advice is to forget it. It's only clutter and dust bunnies. Loving relationships are more important.

But Katrina won't forget it. She burst into my office one day all excited with a new formula. "Oh, you are going to love this," she started. "I learned it last week in a class at the community school. I'm going to reclaim my house finally."

She proudly showed me laminated placards that she had made for each room of the house. On each placard was a description of what the room was used for, to be posted at the doorway of a given room. She reckoned that she could use the placards to remind herself and the family of what activities and stuff belonged in each room. And if a family member got it wrong, she could gently encourage him or her to move to another room.

Visual supports are great, but I'm not sure how long this system lasted. Some time later Barry told me that Katrina wanted him to build a decorative folding screen to place in front of a pile of boxes that were spilling out into the living room. So much for rules – and placards to enforce them!

Creative, or Too Far Outside the Box?

If an Aspie woman can't organize the house, manage child tantrums or modify unusual sleep patterns, she can get distracted with other projects. Barry, Katrina and the children live on a small farm, acreage more accurately, since not one of them takes care of anything. The land is covered with blackberries, and the fences are in disrepair. They have goats, dogs, chickens and horses. The animals get fed and watered, and brushed once in a while. And the stalls in the ratty old barn get mucked out when no one can stand the mess and the smell any more, or when the vet complains that the horses have hoof infections once again.

But it is Katrina's dream to have a farm, and she worked hard to accomplish her dream. While she and Barry can afford this hobby, neither of them comprehends the actual work and organization required to keep such a complex organization running.

"OMG! " Barry exclaimed one day. "You won't believe what Katrina has done now." He was smiling even though his tone was serious. I think it was more of a smirk, like he was finally going to prove that his wife had gone over the edge and that she could no longer blame him for everything.

"What's up?" I asked.

"Katrina has been complaining for a long time that we need to have more family time, like running our farm and 4-H projects is not enough! She says the kids are getting older and we need to have an activity that will be good for teenagers so they will bring their friends by. So you know what happened last week when I was out of town on a business trip? Katrina rented a crew to start building a swimming pool in our pasture. No kidding!"

I am usually not surprised by anything that my clients tell me, but even Barry could see the look of surprise on my face. I was not just curious; there was more. I said, "What do you mean, 'rented a crew'? Do you mean she hired a pool contractor?"

"Nope," he said. "She didn't hire a pool contractor. She thought that would cost too much money. Nope. She rented a backhoe and then hired an excavation crew. They dug this huge pit in the pasture. Right now with the rain, it is filling up with mud." Barry looked horrified – and satisfied at the same time.

I was stunned, which apparently satisfied Barry. "Oh, Barry, I am so sorry. What are you going to do? I mean, Katrina can't think that you can make a swimming pool in the middle of the pasture from a big muddy hole, can she?"

Barry delivered the punch line. "Well no, not now. After the hole was dug, she started calling around to pool contractors and asked them to finish the job and they just laughed at her."

Katrina just can't get it that she is not always able to create what she sees in her mind. People with Asperger's can be marvelously creative. They have the kinds of minds that "think outside the box." For example, Katrina grows a totally organic garden for her family and has taught her children a lot about organic farming and caring for the farm animals. She has an herb garden in her kitchen window so that she can cut fresh herbs for cooking, even though sometimes she forgets to water her plants.

But there are times when Aspies are driven to create and fail to use common sense. The swimming pool is one of those times. Now there is a huge pit in the pasture, less room for the animals to graze, and a potential for a dangerous cave-in, not to mention the cost of repairing the hole. As for what the neighbors will think about the "swimming pool," well . . . they have long ago learned to accept this unusual family. In fact, Barry reports overhearing some neighbors calling his family the Griswolds, referring to the dysfunctional family in the *National Lampoon* movies.

Bipolar or Asperger Syndrome?

Many might say that Katrina's disorganization looks more like bipolar disorder than Asperger's, and there are certainly some similarities. The swimming pool episode smacks of a manic episode. But in general, Katrina's attempts to create a happy family life come from the mistake that so many with Asperger's make. She keeps searching for answers to relating, but she looks outside herself, not within, and certainly not within the other person. She loves her children and her husband dearly, but her lack of empathy makes it hard for her to know what is needed at any moment in time. So she opts for rules and stuff in a desire to make it all look normal.

As a result of constant failure in the family realm, Katrina experiences mounting anxiety and cries at the drop of a hat. It is this increasing anxiety that drives Katrina to search for new and better ways to do life, instead of relaxing into who she really is – a creative woman with Asperger Syndrome.

Another element contributing to Katrina's situation is that she felt abandoned as a child. Because of her unusual style, she was shunned by others as a child and even early in her professional career. Her childhood was chaotic. Undoubtedly, her parents were no better equipped to raise children with Asperger Syndrome than Katrina is. Katrina left her childhood with the determination to make it better for her own children. She is over-protective and projects her childhood distress onto her children. Unfortunately, this is causing even more emotional separation for Katrina and her husband – and some day probably between herself and her children as well.

What's a Woman to Do?

Growing up with a mother who presumably had Asperger Syndrome has helped me a great deal when it comes to understanding women with AS. My mom was extremely practical at times, and at other times she engaged in the most useless behaviors. One of her more brilliant inventions involved using Dad's old cotton dress shirts and redesigning them as summer attire for herself. Made of Oxford cloth, these white shirts were cool when she worked in the yard and also protected her from the sun. This was during the 1950s, before we had all of these modern fibers and sun-protective clothing, but Mom already knew that there was a need for such things. Once again she was ahead of her time.

On the other hand, Mom was fascinated by desert tortoises – a weird sort of hobby. Once when we drove through the Mojave Desert to visit family members who lived near Edwards Air Force Base, Mom decided we needed tortoises as pets. So she collected a couple and brought them home to Oregon, where they were completely out of their element. Not sure what they ate, Mom fed them lettuce. Maybe she caught bugs for them, too. I'll never know. She had my dad build them a pen from plywood, and we kept them in the basement. Once she tried tethering the tortoises so that they could be out in the yard, but where do you tie the tether to a tortoise? She tried it around one of their legs, but the poor things nearly tore off their legs trying to dig into the dirt for protection.

I never asked my mother why she thought this made any sense, but I suppose she thought the family needed a hobby, much like Katrina's swimming pool idea. Eventually, my dad took pity on the poor animals and carted them off to the local zoo, where they remain to this day.

Being an eccentric man is somewhat more acceptable in our society than being an eccentric woman. Who doesn't like the absent-minded professor? But women with this disorder suffer a great deal. They seem more aware than their male counterparts that relationships are important to attend to. They also seem to accept that it is a woman's duty to care for the children, to maintain the household, and in general to keep the family happy and healthy. But they are usually not well equipped to handle this role. Their children view them as pushy and preoccupied. Their spouses view them as anxious and emotionally distant. Their neighbors see them as oddities.

At the very worst, people can get very angry with these women for failing to meet neurotypical (NT) female standards. Thus, Aspie women can become isolated and feel like failures as women, even if successful in their careers.

So what's a woman to do? An AS woman has a lot to accomplish to come to terms with who she is and negotiate a healthy relationship with her partner . . . without many of the requisite empathy skills to accomplish this task. In Katrina's case she has the gender imperative to take responsibility for her marriage and her family, but must work with her AS husband who is often as clueless as she is.

The most important first step for an AS woman is self-acceptance, which does not come from trying to fit in. If a woman with Asperger Syndrome and her family can accept that this is the way it is, they can finally move on to develop a structure to live within. But just like an NT woman, Katrina needs to move on if her "Spousal Unit" will not work with her to find solutions.

Here are some tips for self-acceptance. While there are few role models for being an eccentric woman, they do exist – or you can be one yourself. Stop expecting to fit in, but reach out to others like yourself or those who can accept your uniqueness. Laugh at your foibles. Explore the little-known world of Asperger Syndrome and teach your daughters how to navigate the world from the lessons you have learned. Trust that God does not create junk. You were designed exactly as you should be, albeit part of a minority group. You have gifts to offer although it may not always seem like that to you.

This doesn't mean you have to give up your search for the perfect housekeeping routine or mothering techniques. Just make sure that what you develop works for you. You will alleviate your anxiety and make your home a much calmer and more loving environment, as a result. Hire as much help as you can afford. Use the microwave or cook everything from organic and scratch – it doesn't matter in terms of your self-esteem (although I suppose healthy food that agrees with your Aspie sensitivities can't hurt). What matters is preserving your self-esteem so that you have time to enjoy your loved ones and they you. And with healthy self-esteem and a healthy body, you can also make better use of psychotherapy to learn skills to manage the anxiety and depression that emerges from time to time.

You won't be the first Aspie mom to let go of wanting to fit in. Harriet Beecher Stowe is best known for her classic novel, *Uncle Tom's Cabin*, but did you know that her first book was on the art of housekeeping? The author who changed the way Americans looked at slavery wrote suggestions for nineteenth-century American women on efficient housekeeping. In those days, women were tied to the house because of the labors of cooking and cleaning, so Harriet came up with ways to break out a woman's time for more creative endeavors, such as writing.

Some of her suggestions sound like they came from an Aspie woman. For example, she saw no need for frequent sweeping and dusting, so she suggested wall-to-wall carpet, which she opined would keep down the dust. Likewise, she thought curtains were a waste and required too much laundering. Instead, she suggested arranging potted plants by the windows so that they grew up to partially shield the view from the outside and still let in sunshine. You go, Harriet!

Lessons Learned

1. Many people with Asperger's have sleep disorders and organizational problems that can create extreme anxiety for them.
2. When parenting requires getting into the mind of the child or the mind of the other parent, Aspies often fail and become controlling (or masterminding).
3. Raising children is an art, not a recipe. Go slowly and get advice from parenting professionals.
4. Organizing the mundane, like a household, is difficult for the Asperger mind and is better left to a housekeeper, if possible.
5. Sometimes the creative force of a woman with AS needs a reality check.
6. Women with AS often suffer severe self-esteem problems unless they learn self-acceptance.
7. Seek the support and guidance of a psychologist who is well versed in the double whammy of dealing with being a woman and having Asperger Syndrome.

CHAPTER ELEVEN

No Shame

You are about to meet Jeri, who is a bit further along in her recovery than Helen. Even though Jeri's husband, Emil, has Asperger Syndrome (AS), she has come to accept his idiosyncrasies and looks elsewhere for the type of love and empathy he cannot give her. Using the counterproductive tools of blame and shame is common for those in a neurotypical (NT)-Asperger marriage.

In this chapter you will make progress in your healing when you take back your life from blame and shame.

Letting Go of Shame and Blame

Co-dependency and abuse can develop in an Asperger-NT relationship when there is a lack of understanding and acceptance of the disorder. The only way to stop the cycle of abuse is to detach and to seek professional help. But you need more than the basics on quelling abusive relationships. You need to educate yourself about the "science" behind AS and the behaviors that result from this developmental disorder (such as those defective mirror neurons that explain so much of the Aspie mind blindness and lack of empathy). With this knowledge comes acceptance of the disorder, which makes it easier to develop methods for both NTs and Aspies to use to keep calm in the face of the emotional flare-ups that result from misunderstanding each other's worlds.

Shame and blame are both examples of misunderstanding as they relate to AS. It is not blame to acknowledge the role of AS in abusive relationships. And there is no shame in making mistakes – even big ones. Instead of shame and blame, it is time to build a context for communicating and loving across the realities – if that is your goal. And even if your goal is to take back your life whether or not your Asperger loved one joins you in the process, or to be a more compassionate NT parent of children with AS, a deeper understanding of the Aspie way of mind can free you from many misconceptions and counterproductive behaviors you have developed about yourself in relationship to your AS loved ones.

It Could Be Them

Jeri beamed when she walked into the room. I noticed right away that she was not wearing her wig. She looked much younger and very stylish with her curly light-brown hair cropped close to her head.

"Dr. Marshack, do you notice anything different about me?" Jeri beamed.

"Of course. You're not wearing your wig." I smiled a broad smile that matched Jeri's. It was good to see her so excited. She had been through so much since she was diagnosed with breast cancer. She had done well during the surgery and treatments, hardly missing any work and still managing to take care of her family and her husband. She even continued to babysit her new granddaughter once a week (most of the time). What a trooper!

Jeri continued. "Yes, but that's not all. My doctor cleared me and told me that I am now officially in remission! To celebrate I decided to shed the wig and color my hair. What do you think?"

"You look beautiful; absolutely beautiful," I said. "I don't think you should let your hair grow any longer. It makes you look radiant and years younger. Keep it short. It's so cute." Jeri beamed with pleasure.

"So what did your husband say about the transformation?" I continued.

Jeri's face changed dramatically, her radiant smile withering. "Oh, Dr. Marshack, you won't believe this – well maybe you will, considering that you know Emil. I didn't tell the kids or Emil that I was coloring my hair or that I didn't want to wear a wig any more. The wig just isn't me, and neither is gray hair. I may have had breast cancer, but my recovery makes me feel young. I want to celebrate. But you know Emil."

Jeri shares the story.

When I got home from the doctor's office, I said, "Emil, I got a good report from the doctor today. I am through with treatments, and the doctor said that I am officially in remission. How about if we go to dinner to celebrate?" You know, Dr. Marshack, Emil never went with me to the medical appointments. Well maybe one or two, but mostly he just ignored me. He was excellent around the house taking care of stuff, but he ignored ME!

So any way, Emil's response to this major news was, "I don't want to think about the cancer any more. What's to celebrate? We've been through enough. Let's drop it. Let's put it behind us and move on."

I was so crushed I couldn't see straight. All I wanted to do was to curl up under the covers and sleep away the day like I used to so that I didn't have to face being married to this guy. I know that he loves me, but this Asperger's thing is too much. I don't think it is unreasonable to ask that he take me to dinner to celebrate that I conquered cancer and that I am going to live. Maybe some flowers, too. Is that too much?

Anyway, I didn't crawl under the covers! I'm done with being so depressed I want to die. I am alive, and I want to have adventures. So for starters, I decided to take off my cancer wig and color my hair. Like I said, I didn't tell Emil or the kids that I was doing it. I wanted to surprise them all. I was hoping this would make a bit of difference and that they would be happy for me. Oh my gosh, you won't believe what happened.

A sly smile crept across her face, and there was a twinkle in her eyes, so I knew there was more to the story. I let my shoulders drop to let the tension drain out. I took in a deep breath as I suddenly noticed that I had not been breathing.

I invited the kids and their wives to dinner after I colored my hair. And when everyone was there, I came out of the bedroom without my wig.

So, "Hi, guys! What do you think of Mom's new do?"

Emil immediately said, "I like the wig better."

Eric, who is just like his dad, you know, said, "Oh, I like your gray hair better; I was used to it."

Ethan looked at me with a big, big, big smile, held both thumbs up and said, "Cool, Mom, cool!" What a sweetheart. At least I know that one of my sons can relate.

And the girls . . . oh my gosh, they were so cute. Ethan's wife gave me a big hug and said, "Let's go shopping this weekend, Mom, and buy you some new things to go with your new look."

And Ariel, poor thing, she ignored Eric and asked if she could join us at the mall.

Jeri started to laugh after telling this story. She was watching me carefully, and when she laughed, I joined her. What a success story. Jeri had originally come to me to help her deal with severe depression that kept her housebound for days, curled up in bed with migraine headaches and not much will to live.

Once I discovered that her husband and youngest son had Asperger Syndrome (both were diagnosed by their respective psychologists), I could help Jeri make sense of her depression. She was so relieved. She finally had an answer to her depression. At least some of the problems weren't hers. It could be them. As hard as it was to accept, her years of depression could be due to her husband's (and son's) inability to connect. And Jeri was caught in the middle.

Sadly, during the course of our therapy, Jeri discovered that she had breast cancer. However, she used her recent discovery of AS to bolster her skills. She read books on Asperger's and books on breast cancer. She joined a cancer recovery group and shared her story of Asperger's and cancer.

She tackled her co-dependency and stopped taking the blame for everything. She gathered old and new friends around her. Even neighbors came to help. One of those neighbors was a breast cancer survivor. They became particularly close, and it was this woman who shared many of the medical appointments with Jeri that Emil refused to go to. And it was this neighbor who took Jeri out to celebrate her success with conquering cancer.

Even though Jeri wanted to celebrate her success with her husband and children, she understood that they weren't rejecting her. Emil just couldn't understand why she wanted to celebrate the cancer. He could not put it together that she wanted to celebrate her triumph over cancer (not the cancer) and her determination to start a life anew. Many people with Asperger's are caught in the world of facts and figures and miss those special defining moments of life. As far as Emil was concerned, the cancer was cured and the family moves on. Why celebrate a normal process?

Always in Charge

Back to Helen.

"I don't look worse for the wear, do I?"

Helen was calm and perfect in every way. She sat comfortably in my office, not a hair out of place – even her nails were manicured. "I know you were worried about me. I am sorry I didn't call. It's just that I had a lot of thinking to do. In some ways I wish that Grant had left me in jail. I was kind of looking forward to getting away from it all for a few days, but I would have been scared stiff for the kids, alone with their dad and worrying about me. He doesn't know how to comfort them, even though he loves them. I know he loves them."

Helen continues almost without taking a breath. "Jasmine was so sweet when I got home. She asked if she could rub my shoulders. She knows that I love that kind of tenderness. And I think it makes her feel useful, so I let her do it . . . and, you know, it did feel good. She has so much trouble relating to others, but she can at least give me a neck rub. That's her way of loving me, an Asperger way."

Helen weaves a new thread into her story. "I saw the wariness in Jason's eyes, though. He watched his father and me very carefully. I had let him down. I should have handled things better so that he didn't have to call the police. It is not up to Jason to protect me. And it was hideous that the children watched me handcuffed and stuffed into the cop car. Will they ever get over that?"

Helen gets animated as her story unfolds.

That night was bad. I heard Jason screaming, "Stop it, Dad! Stop kicking Jasmine!" I ran to the kitchen as fast as I could. Jason was standing there squaring off with his father. Grant looked livid. He turned that wild-eyed look at me.

"Don't you interfere! I can handle this," he said. "Don't you interfere. I'm disciplining the kids. Jason just jumped me!"

Jason interrupted, "But, Mom, Dad slugged me. He was kicking Jasmine and she was crying, standing there crying unable to protect herself. I tried to stop him, but he turned on me and slammed me to the wall."

"Grant, did you kick Jasmine? Is that true?" I asked.

"Yes, it's true, but she started it! And now you are interfering and making matters worse!" Grant's eyes were black with rage. When he's angry, all you can see are those black eyes, like there is nothing but the pupils showing. His lips were narrow and pressed against each other tightly and the muscles in his cheeks twitched, as if he was so angry that he could not speak.

"How could you?" I burst out. "Did you punch Jason, too? For goodness sake. They are only children."

Grant explains, "But Jasmine started it. She was mad that I told her to clean up the kitchen. She yelled at me 'No!' I reached out to grab her and make her come back to the kitchen, and then she turned and kicked me. It was a reflex. I kicked her back. Then before I knew it, Jason jumped me from behind. I didn't mean to. But what was I to do? He jumped me, so I took a swing at him and I guess I connected."

Helen looks at me as if to seek approval as she continues.

"Oh Grant, how could you? They are only children. Of course, they start these things. That's what kids do. They aren't grown up yet and they often are irrational. Kids are kids. And you know that Jasmine is special. It's hard for her to make transitions and to deal with stress, especially when she didn't expect to clean the kitchen. Good grief! You're the grownup. You can make better choices than this."

Grant glowered at me. "I wish you wouldn't interfere. I can handle this. Now see what you are doing? Jasmine is upset all over again." Jasmine was crying and pleading with me to leave Daddy alone.

I tried to comfort Jasmine. "Jasmine, honey, please go to your room. Mommy will be there in a minute. Please go to your room. Grant, don't move. I'll be right back. Please sit down. Jason, go to your room. I will be there in a minute."

"What are you going to tell them? Don't undermine me!" Grant looked fierce, like he was trapped and would jump me if I got in his way. I got very calm inside and told him to sit down again.

"I won't undermine you, Grant. I'm going to calm the children down and will be right back to talk with you about what happened. No sense in everyone being upset. Let me handle this."

I left Grant alone in the kitchen while I went in to comfort the children.

"Jasmine, sweetheart, are you O.K.?" I reached out for my little girl to comfort her.

"Yes, Mommy, but Daddy kicked me!" Tears were streaming down her cheeks, and there was a look of disbelief on her face.

"I know, sweetheart. Daddy is very angry. Daddy should not kick you, even if you kicked him first. Daddy is a grownup and should never act that way. But we have to learn to stay out of Daddy's way if he is angry. It's better that way. Can you do that from now on?" Jasmine nodded, but I'm not sure she really can do what I asked.

Then I headed over to Jason's room, but he wasn't there. Just then, I heard another outburst from Grant. "You little bastard. I don't want to see your damned face! Get back to your room!" I ran to the kitchen only to find Grant shoving Jason back toward his room. I lost it. I just lost it! I lunged for Grant and slapped him in the face, knocking off his glasses, which went sailing across the kitchen. I couldn't believe I did it. Honestly, it was so weird; like it was in slow motion.

"Grant, stop it!" I screamed. Then in defiance I stomped on his glasses, shattering them into pieces. (Gosh, the floor is a mess too, all cut up. I like that flooring. I hope I can replace it.) [That's Helen . . . even in a crisis she can think about replacing her kitchen flooring.] *But I wanted to do more. I wanted to gouge out his eyes, I was so furious.*

Grant was stunned. He just stood there. He has ever seen me get so violent before. Yes, I have yelled at him, but never taken a swing at him. He just stood there, looking at me with that blank look. And then . . . he sat down and everything stopped. Well, sort of. I guess Jason called the police when I took a swing at his father.

Oh my God, dealing with the police was a trip! They didn't want to hear anything I had to say. They wouldn't listen to the children either. All they were interested in was that I hit Grant and that his glasses were broken. They decided on the spot that I was the aggressor and, therefore, should be arrested. Grant didn't say a word. He didn't defend me. He just sat there speechless. Jason tried, bless his soul, but the police believed the child was protecting his mother, so off I went to the hooskow!

Returning to the present, Helen continued, "Thank you for being there when Jason called, or I would have been in jail for days. Thank you also for giving Grant the name of an attorney. He has been very helpful over the last couple of days, but the expense is something else. How do attorneys get away with charging these fees any way?" That's Helen . . . always the survivor . . . always multitasking . . . but not in touch with her feelings of fear and anguish – not yet.

I finally broke into Helen's monologue. I knew that she needed to tell her story, but I realized that there was another purpose behind these stories – to stay in control. If I was ever to help Helen, she had to learn that she could ask for help instead of having all of the answers, all of the time. She has multitasked for years and analyzes everything. With no one to lean on at home, she has learned to detach and analyze and come up with solutions and defer her emotions and needs for some later date, which never comes.

"Helen, please listen to me. What you have been through is very traumatic. I realize that you have a lot to take care of. The children need you right now. Grant needs you. But please, let me help. You don't have to do this all alone."

Helen looked at me with that same stare that I presume Grant showed her – blank. Then she began to cry as the realization set in.

"Thank you," she said, suddenly looking small. "I feel so alone. I feel like no one understands what I live with. I feel so mixed up about it all. My precious daughter, Jasmine. I grieve for her. Life is hard and she is so misunderstood. There is a beautiful person inside her that is all locked up. And Jason, he is trying to take care of everything, just like me. But Grant, what am I supposed to do about Grant? I feel so guilty. I have failed to help them. I exploded and caused all of this heartache. I mean, I know that Grant hit the kids and that has to stop. But my exploding and hitting him back is not the answer. I should have done better."

"Helen, stop blaming yourself. You have been dealing with Asperger Syndrome alone for so many years that it has worn you down. It is no one's fault, really. In some ways it is my fault, and the fault of my profession, that we still do not entirely understand this syndrome and how to help families cope with the strain it can bring. Please don't feel ashamed for what happened. You snapped under the pressure. You are a strong woman. You have taken such good care of your family, but there is only so much that one person can do alone. We need to build up your reserves so that you won't snap again. It's time to get regular support and big, huge breaks from it all so that you can be there for you and those you love."

It is a very sad fact in this age of mandatory domestic violence arrest procedures that women are frequently arrested when they stand up for themselves against an abusive mate. After suffering oppressive abuse for many years, a woman may finally stand up for herself or her children, as we saw in Helen's case. She may resist an assault or strike first to protect herself or her children from a perceived attack. Not only are many psychologists unaware, but the police and the courts are not well educated about this type of domestic violence either. While self-defense is legal, the police are still very likely to arrest the person causing the injury or damage in the moment, ignoring the long-standing abuse a woman like Helen has suffered. Later the victim of long-term domestic violence has to prove her innocence in court or plead guilty and accept a suspended sentence for a year or two. The shame and disruption to the family is intense. Plus this does a disservice to the abusive/controlling partner who learns nothing and takes no responsibility for his part in this destructive drama.

Accepting and Allowing Brings Healing

I wish I could say that all it took was this one conversation to get Helen to take the steps she needed in order to get well. But it took many more months before Helen could let go of the shame of being arrested and putting her family through this turmoil.

Taking responsibility for others is what she has done for years. Because they are all so vulnerable – Grant, Jasmine and Jason – Helen has stepped up to the plate and handled their responsibilities for them, leaving her in the unenviable position of being the target of their frustrations, too. For example, every time Helen took charge and showed her strength, she made Grant feel small and he subsequently got upset.

A few short months later, after Helen got through the ordeal of the arrest, she had this to say. (Fortunately, because Grant refused to testify against her, the state dropped the charges.)

"Dr. Marshack, I can't believe I told Jasmine to stay out of her Dad's way. I can't believe I told her to humor him when he is angry. That's what I have been doing for years, and that is not a life. That is co-dependency, just like you have explained over and over. Has it come to this that my life is nothing more than walking on eggshells around Grant? And now I am teaching the children to do the same. I sound like some pathetic abused wife. Is that what I am?"

I agreed. "Actually, yes you are. It's not that Grant wants to be abusive, any more than Jasmine does. But Jasmine and Grant are not getting the professional guidance they need to moderate their intense feelings and their confusion about how relationships work. All of you need to learn better strategies for coping with stress. Grant and Jasmine need to learn to tame their noisy brains and their low tolerance for anxiety. You and Jason need to learn to translate your world for the other two. They have a lot of difficulty understanding what motivates NTs."

I continued to reassure Helen.

"Remember when I told you about mirror neurons? Those interconnective neurons in the brain that are in short demand for Aspies? Those neurons that communicate the unspoken to different parts of the brain? Those neurons that fire off when an NT looks into another person's face and just knows what he or she is thinking? Those neurons that are responsible for an NT's empathy?

"Well, Grant and Jasmine have a hard time understanding the nonverbal cues that you and Jason find the essence of communication. And they also have a hard time empathizing with you. They know what they feel, but they can't easily put themselves in your shoes because those mirror neurons are not working well for them. It's time for you and Jason to learn to explain yourselves in more detail. It's time for you to stop taking it so personally when Jasmine doesn't get it. It's time for you to let Grant be who he is and not expect more than he can give."

Helen seemed to be listening to me in a new way, and I continue to explain. "This is a lot of work and it may not be enough for you, but this is your family. You love them. They love you. And it's time to stop the anger, the hurt and the violence."

I am not sure what Helen will do in the long run. She complains that Grant feels to her more like a third child than a husband. She complains that she would like a "real" husband to talk to, to share her life with. She complains that raising the children by herself is tiring. But she is a committed wife and mother, and I doubt that she would feel comfortable leaving this marriage while the children are still in the home. Even though she has said she wants a divorce, she has no plan. It is an idea that may or may not develop over time. If she can learn to detach from her notions of the ideal marriage, she may come to love and cherish Grant for what he can offer.

On the other hand, Grant needs to commit to his growth, too. As a man with Asperger Syndrome, he needs to face the reality that he would be a challenge for any NT woman. He needs to understand that Helen is not overreacting. She is grieving deeply over the loss of a partner who can empathize with her and know who she is at the deepest level. Most NT women dream of marrying their soulmate. Grant may love Helen, but without those mirror neurons working well, he does not know her. They are not soul mates. That is an important distinction.

For all couples dealing with a mate with Asperger Syndrome, the bottom line is this. First, you must accept the other for who he or she is. Second, you must allow for differences. If you insist that your mate be just like you and understand you without explanation, you will fail. NTs must develop the Aspie vocabulary and detach from all of those notions of a soulmate. Chances are your Asperger mate loves you but has no way to convey that except through the work he or she does. This is a chance for NT partners to learn to accept that they are loved even without the typical demonstrations of love that are so precious to the NT way of life. None of this is easy, but it is the way.

Lessons Learned

1. It is normal for an NT to ask of Aspie loved ones that they consider your feelings or think of loving things to do for you, but you will have to instruct them on how to so. They cannot read your mind.
2. If you are depressed, it could be "them," not you. This is not to blame, but to look at the source of your depression.
3. Do you always need to be in charge? Always multitasking to keep up with the demands of your family? If so, this is another aspect of co-dependency, and it will sap your energy.
4. Don't be caught up in the drama of it all. You are more than a survivor. Take a break and rediscover yourself.
5. Step out of the cycle of abuse. Stop walking on eggshells. Get into therapy and insist that your spouse go, too.
6. Those with Asperger Syndrome need to recognize that untreated AS often leads to abuse. Stop the cycle of abuse by seeking psychotherapy for your "noisy" brain and your anxiety.
7. Accept your spouse for who he or she is and nothing more. Detachment is freedom from abuse and depression.
8. Your compassion will grow and your depression will wane when you learn to speak your spouse's language.

CHAPTER TWELVE

Divorce Wars

Like Chapter Six on sex, this chapter is a sensitive one. It is not easy to face the prospect of divorce, but there are times when divorce is the only answer. Whether the divorce is friendly, business-like or high-conflict, you need to be prepared so that you cause as little damage to yourself and your loved ones as possible. That's about as positive as it gets, I'm afraid.

This chapter takes a close look at divorce – the good, the bad and the ugly. Taking the high road and being willing to detach from your pride makes it possible to leave with dignity. After that, you start to rebuild from the wreckage.

When Divorce Is the Only Answer

It is uncomfortable for me as a psychologist to write about how to get a divorce when I work so hard to help people mend their marriages and keep their families intact. But there are times when divorce is the only answer. While Helen chooses to stay in her marriage, at least a while longer, other neurotypicals (NTs) decide to leave.

Please don't let anyone convince you that divorce can be easy or painless. And in the case of an Asperger's (AS) divorce, remember that the lack of connectedness that forced the issue in the first place will make communicating even harder during a breakup.

Contempt of Court

The following is an example from my own divorce to demonstrate the conflict between the best interests of a family and our adversarial court system.

I sat in the courtroom in utter disbelief that the judge had just ordered both of my children to appear at the court hearing the next day. I was in the middle of a divorce from my husband of twenty-three years and it was going very badly.

In a power play, the judge (a long-time colleague of my ex-husband, and the ex-wife of my lawyer) ordered me to bring my children to court so she could interrogate them. The girls, aged twelve and fifteen at the time, were already traumatized by their parents' high-conflict divorce, so it was beyond my comprehension that the judge would put them through more torment by forcing them to take sides in the courtroom.

If I didn't bring the girls to court the next day, I would be found in contempt of court and fined, put in jail or lose temporary custody of my children. If I brought them, how would I ever help them heal from one more emotional assault? My ex-husband (a divorce attorney himself) was in full agreement with the judge about bringing the girls into this snake pit. Obviously, I could not count on him to protect them. So I did the only thing a mother could do – neither the girls nor I showed up for court.

High-Conflict Divorce

There were many, many more incidents like this in my two-year battle to get a divorce. In spite of the suffering, and even the terror of the legal process, the divorce taught me a lot about what many of my clients go through, so in one way it was useful. The suffering of a high-conflict divorce is not something that resolves quickly, especially if there are children involved. I suspect that my children and I will deal with symptoms of post-traumatic stress for years to come.

What makes a high-conflict divorce? Why did my divorce end up in this category when I am a professional psychologist? Why on earth would a domestic relations judge (and a woman) be so insensitive to the needs of children? Is there another way to get couples to resolve their divorces more amicably? While there are no easy answers, I hope to answer these tough questions in a moment.

Nowadays when a woman, or a man, tells me that she or he is afraid to get a divorce, I have a new perspective. I know firsthand how damaging a divorce can be. Not all divorces are as hostile as mine, but unfortunately divorcing an Aspie can be. Sheila Linehan, a Canadian attorney, has written widely on high-conflict divorce (see "High Conflict & Asperger's Syndrome" at www.mediate.com). Although not a mental health specialist, Linehan speculates that a high preponderance of high-conflict divorces includes at least one Asperger member in the dyad. My experience with many clients over the years leads me to agree.

There are many reasons for this, but it can't all be laid on the Aspie partner. It is an interaction that is fueled by the NT as much as the Aspie. As you have seen in other chapters, Asperger Syndrome can lead the NT spouse or family member to extreme despair. People don't make the best choices when they are depressed, lonely and desperate. Often the NT is critical of the poor social and communication skills of the Aspie partner. Sometimes the NT throws tantrums. By the time divorce is considered, the marital pair may be at extreme odds with each other, and reasonable solutions do not even cut through the anger and pain – hence the high conflict.

Lack of Empathy Can Lead to Divorce

Briefly, here are the stories of Heather, Evie, Andrea, Molly, Justine, Gary, Greta and Carolyn, all of whom are pondering divorce from an AS mate. All their divorces have the potential to be high-conflict. It all depends upon what the NT partners do next.

It is not necessary to divorce an Asperger mate. It is not a fact that all people with AS contribute to a high-conflict divorce. However, it is definitely something to add to the mix when considering a divorce, primarily because it is so difficult for the AS mate to empathize with his or her partner. This disability in the area of empathy intensifies under the pressure of a marriage that is falling apart, just as any of us psychologically and physically deteriorates under stress. If one of the reasons the NT spouse is considering divorce is the lack of reciprocity in the relationship with the Aspie spouse, it is not reasonable to think the Aspie partner will do any better during the divorce. Usually the opposite is the case.

Heather. Heather was suffering agony in her marriage. "Dr. Marshack, Arnie tells me that he will take the children from me if I file for divorce. He has said this before. I don't want to fight over our children, but I feel I will die if I have to stay in this marriage!"

Heather has a number of health issues that are probably related to her eighteen years of marriage to a recently diagnosed AS mate. You can't blame Heather's husband for her illnesses. It's just that years of "just not getting it" causes incredible stress for both, and stress can lead to illness. Heather has aches and pains in every joint, but the doctor cannot find arthritis. She is prone to headaches. She has had overactive Candida bacteria in her digestive tract, leaving her tired and feeling as if her skin is on fire.

Further, TMJ (muscle and joint problems in her jaw) developed recently when Heather had some dental work. All of these small but painful illnesses weaken Heather emotionally, and emotional distress adds to the physical pain. It is a vicious cycle. Ultimately, these illnesses can create a lifetime of disability or lead to more serious disease.

Evie. Evie has stayed for over thirty years with a man who doesn't know her. He has no friends. He works, sleeps, eats, watches TV and not much else. "Can it be possible that Duane is really this cut off? Our kids are raised. The mortgage is paid. We are set for retirement, but there is no love here and no zest for life. I don't know what he will do if I leave him."

Many in Evie's situation do leave, and their AS mate accepts the divorce quietly. Sometimes he lives the rest of his life without a partner. Frequently, he marries the first woman who offers. After all, marriage to this type of man is an "arrangement of convenience." Duane is not very deep in that area.

Andrea. Andrea is much more concerned and frightened about divorce than Heather and Evie. She is a professional woman married to a prominent judge. As an attorney herself, Andrea knows what her husband could do to ruin her life. He could make it impossible for her ever to work again. He could even go so far as to alienate their children, regardless of how damaging this would be to them. Andrea has seen him take revenge on others, and it frightens her to think of that maliciousness being directed at her.

Then there are the children – young teens, who love their father even though they don't connect much with him. One has been diagnosed with Asperger Syndrome like his father. Andrea grieves for this child. What will he think about his own prognosis and future relationships if Andrea leaves his father?

On top of this, Andrea is dreadfully overweight. "Honestly, I don't think there is anything I can do until the children are grown and I have enough saved to retire. Until then I eat, work and try to get a break once in a while with my friends."

Molly. Molly decided to have affairs; several over the years. "Well, you know it is easier that way until I fall in love with some guy. Then, of course, I struggle with my choice to stay in the marriage. Martin never, ever, suspects I am having an affair because he believes he is in charge of everything. I feel horrible. Am I bad? This is not what I want for my life or my kids. But Martin controls the money, the kids and me. We have a prenuptial agreement. The only way I could leave Martin is with only the clothes on my back. He would not only keep the kids but withhold my underwear, too!"

Justine. Justine was willing to take the risk. She bundled up her little ones, rented a small, furnished house nearby and moved out one day when Edwin was out of town. She is not keeping anything a secret. She expects child support but nothing else. Edwin can keep everything in their home, even the children's furnishings. Predictably, Edwin has locked down the bank accounts, changed the locks on the doors and is withholding even grocery money, pending litigation. Justine doesn't care.

She says, "I am free to find my true self again. Living with a man who will not let me be free is not living. I'll figure out something. I have family and friends who can help. I can work. Mom offered to babysit. I haven't worked in ten years, and even then I worked for a small salary, but I don't care. I have lost ten pounds in the month I've been gone and haven't felt better in my life. I've been making phone calls for jobs, and so far I have created three interviews. Not bad. The kids miss Daddy, but he refuses to visit unless I come back home. What an idiot! I would be happy to have the kids visit with him. I don't even care if he gives me a dime, but don't tell that to my attorney!" Justine winks at me, obviously still riding high with her recent decision. I am not sure she fully realizes how difficult things could get over the next few weeks and months, but she is committed to starting a new life.

Gary. Finally, the proverbial straw broke the camel's back for Gary. Raven had been irresponsible so many times, even endangering the children with her immature ways. But this time, he decided it was over. Gary came home from work one day to find a note from Raven, his Aspie wife. She wrote that she had a "bad day" and had decided to take herself to the movies to unwind and that she would be home at midnight or so.

So what's the problem? Everyone needs a mental health break once in a while. True, but in this case, Raven left their two children, aged six and ten, home alone for more than three hours. The kids were fine. They had cereal for dinner, watched TV and waited for Daddy to come home . . . and take care of things.

Gary decided then and there to get a divorce, but he feels guilty because he knows that Raven doesn't mean to be irresponsible. He can endure a cluttered house and cereal for dinner. He loves his wife's quirky sense of humor. He can even accept that the young kids can manage for a bit by themselves, even though it can be frightening at times. But he knows that he and the children need more from a mom and a lover than Raven can give.

Greta. I noticed Greta limping into my office one morning wearing a prosthetic boot. "Are you O.K.?" I blurted out before I even said "good morning." My simple expression of concern brought Greta to tears. This is a pretty common reaction from mates who get little verbal emotional support from their AS partners.

"Didn't Gaylord tell you when he came in last week?" She looked pained and stunned. "I know you have recommended that I hang in there and learn his language. I know you have told me that Gaylord loves me even if he has a hard time connecting. I watch him make efforts, too. But I am frightened, and I just don't know if it is even safe for me to stay in this marriage."

Apparently, Gaylord and Greta had been hiking with friends a couple of weeks earlier when Greta stumbled, fell down a ravine and broke her ankle. Gaylord made an effort to rescue his wife but was so upset that others had to step in – good thing that there were others in their hiking party. Even after Greta was carried back to the path and down to the car, Gaylord didn't know what to do. One of Greta's friends offered to drive her to the hospital, so Gaylord let her do that. In the meantime he remained behind to continue the afternoon hike! After all, Greta was being taken care of; he assumed she would have asked him to go along if she needed him. He didn't even call the hospital or the girlfriend to check on his wife. To make matters worse, he got home before Greta, who had to wait in the emergency room for hours. When Greta finally got home, Gaylord was fast asleep since he had to get up for work the next day.

Carolyn. Carolyn summed it up well when she broke through the dilemma of choosing herself over her husband of forty years. At sixty-two, Carolyn decided to get a divorce. The kids were raised and now raising their own children. The guilt Carolyn felt over abandoning her husband and her marital commitment melted away one day with the following realization. "I woke up and realized that I'm not leaving Roger because he is bad, because he's not. I'm leaving Roger because there's no reason to stay."

Like Helen, these NT partners are pondering divorce because they have lost track of their values and their true selves. But they are caught in the dilemma of doing what is best for them, yet caring for their spouses and the children that they have reared together. They don't want to make that difficult decision of choosing themselves over others. This is a painful choice, especially when the reason for the spouse's behavior is a developmental disorder. It is one thing to divorce a thoughtless, insensitive narcissist-like controlling partner. It is quite another to divorce a person who doesn't even know that he/she is causing harm.

Three Kinds of Divorces

Two things make a high-conflict divorce possible – motive and means. Many people view their divorce as high-conflict because it is stressful and because there are conflicts and confrontation. But the truth is that very few divorces are high-conflict in the strict sense of this term. In my professional experience, I have seen three kinds of divorce scenarios.

- **Business-like divorce.** The parties recognize that they are no longer in love, maybe never were, and want to go their separate ways. So they part amicably and, unless there are children, they have little contact in the future. If there are children, they handle things fairly and respectfully in order to provide quality parenting for their children.
- **Friendly divorce.** This couple recognizes that they probably would have made better friends than sweethearts, so the parting is amicable. Often these couples remain friends and share parenting comfortably with each other and with any future spouses. When people hear about this kind of divorce, they are surprised, but in truth about one third of couples have a friendly divorce.
- **High-conflict divorce.** Unfortunately, this type of couple cannot resolve their differences in either a business-like or in a friendly way. They create a war that is costly and damaging to the children and to themselves. In fact, the damage they wreak spreads a wide net into their extended families and friends, and sometimes even into the greater community. In the long run, this couple pays the price because they may never be able to restore their lives to healthy functioning.

Controlling People

Before getting to the motive and means behind high-conflict divorce, let's take a little detour to better understand the type of person who usually initiates a high-conflict divorce, whether Asperger

Syndrome is involved or not. Author Patricia Evans[5] calls them "controlling people."

In a nutshell, controlling people tend to be narcissistic and low on empathy. Such a person acts as if she is the center of the universe. In her eyes, her beliefs are the "right" ones. Her perspective is the "right one." Her actions are the "right ones."

A natural outcome of the narcissistic-like personality is a lack of empathy for others. While the person is well aware of her feelings, she has no concept of how the other feels. When you don't know how another person feels, it is extremely difficult to understand the other's beliefs, perspectives or actions. Therefore, a person with these kinds of characteristics is often negative and critical of the other if he disagrees.

Loving relationships require empathy to mature. If you have empathy for your spouse, you know how he feels. This means you can relate to his beliefs, perspectives and actions, even if you do not agree. If you can relate, you can be respectful and kind. Being able to step into another's shoes is vital to a healthy relationship and makes love grow. There is an added advantage of being able to understand our lover's mind. Because he is different than we are, our sweetheart in life helps us to see things in new ways – ways we could never have understood without empathy.

The other ingredient for a high-conflict divorce is the controlling person's counterpart, a person who works for equality in relationships. This type of person is often very nurturing and self-effacing, and has a strong sense of justice. Thus, while the controlling person works toward a win-lose solution to problems, the nurturing or egalitarian person works for a win-win. According to Patricia Evans, this places the win-win person at a disadvantage. While the egalitarian person keeps empathizing with the controlling person in an effort to create a win-win solution, the controlling person views this behavior as weak and an opportunity to conquer.

Essentially, the controlling person creates a power struggle with the unwitting egalitarian. This keeps the egalitarian on the hook, so

---

[5] *The Verbally Abusive Relationship,* (1996). Cincinnati, OH: Adams Media.

to speak, because she can't seem to realize that she will never create a win-win solution with a controlling person. Sadly, it appears to be true that people with controlling and narcissist-like tendencies marry egalitarians and create high-conflict divorces all too often.

For example, Justine recalls a rather mild incident where she and Edwin were arguing. In an effort to get Edwin to consider another point of view, Justine pointed out to him, "You think other people should think like you do, don't you?" Edwin gave her his characteristic flat look and without skipping a beat said, "Why yes, I do." As long as Edwin has that point of view, there is no reason for Justine to argue another view. She will lose.

Also, we have seen what happened to Justine when she moved out and filed for divorce. Edwin couldn't see her actions as anything other than winning and retaliated by locking her out financially in order to get even. Win/lose. It is a destructive game.

Andrea, on the other hand, has a more serious situation to contend with. Her partner is a judge and in a position to create extreme destruction in her life. When she tries to bring up her point of view, her husband dismisses her with comments like, "You can't prove that!" as if each argument is a matter of law instead of a matter of opinion or negotiating a compromise. Andrea understands all too well that if she should file for divorce, her husband will come unglued. He will perceive her as having the upper hand and could retaliate with force, something that frightens Andrea into submission to protect herself and her children.

While not all Aspies are controlling people to the extreme degree demonstrated by Edwin or Andrea's husband, the concrete or black-and-white thinking that is so characteristic of Asperger's can contribute to unethical and controlling behavior. If they feel rejected by their spouse, Aspies can cast the other person in the role of villain and feel justified fighting back in the most unkind and unjust ways.

Not all people with AS are narcissists, of course. Even with the empathy problem, many people with Asperger's have strong values regarding how to treat others. In therapy, they can be walked through the situation and come to understand why their partner wants a divorce, or better yet, they can come to learn how to resolve problems with their spouse. But if a spouse with Asperger's does not have solid values and abandons the high road in favor of winning at all costs, the outcome for a family can be disastrous.

For example, Justine was to learn much later how distressed her husband could become. When she would not return home as he expected, Edwin began spreading rumors that she was dangerous and crazy. He filed for custody of the children and included in court documents that Justine was unstable and unfit because she had moved out of their home impulsively and with very little money. He also implied that there was another man.

These attacks put Justine in the position of having to defend herself and protect her children from the lies. Obviously, she felt terrorized by her husband. Unable to understand why Justine would leave him, and unwilling to get professional psychotherapy, Edwin eventually deteriorated to the level of paranoia where he did not trust most anyone anymore. This is a sad consequence of the black-and-white thinking of some with Asperger's.

Justine was shocked when she went to drop off the children for a visit with their father, only to find that she could not get to the front door because Edwin had padlocked the courtyard gate with a bicycle lock. The children were crying and confused, and it was all that Justine could do to calm them down and drive back home. All the while she was worried that the judge would take away the children because she didn't leave them in the driveway for their court-ordered visit.

Was Edwin shutting out Justine and the children or was he locking himself in . . . and away from the world that was too painful and confusing for him? Either way, all parties suffer tremendously.

Motive and Means

Personality alone is not enough to create a high-conflict divorce. The partners also need means and motive.

"Means" generally equates to money and/or power. If one or both parties have enough money to wage a war and are not concerned with an unhealthy outcome (or not aware of this possibility), the result is likely a high-conflict divorce. Generally, healthy people quit the conflict when they recognize that they are throwing their money away. Only those snared by the narcissistic-like power struggle continue to the "death."

Another source of means is power, which can come in a variety of forms. Being a divorce attorney is a source of power. Having a personal relationship with the judge is a source of power. Being personally acquainted with the local police and the city prosecutor helps. Being famous or having media connections is a source of power. All of these things can be used to create a high-conflict divorce.

A third source of means is being irrational and tenacious. Even without money or power, a person can create a high-conflict divorce through simple means. There is an axiom that the most irrational and inconsistent person in the system is in control of the system because he doesn't follow the rules. If the controlling person is uncooperative, antagonistic or dishonorable, a high-conflict divorce will take shape.

Then there is "motive." If a person feels aggrieved and is totally controlling, he can feel justified doing just about anything to trash and burn the other person. This includes dragging the couple's children into the fray. And no matter how self-effacing the egalitarian is, he or she will fight back if pushed far enough. Thus, the motive to protect and defend is aroused. Unfortunately, trying to fight a narcissist is like dousing yourself with gasoline and lighting yourself on fire.

Solutions to High-Conflict Divorce

In spite of this disheartening look at high-conflict divorce, I still believe it is possible to prevent, or at least better tolerate, a high-conflict divorce. Anyone going through a life-changing experience like a divorce, high-conflict or otherwise, should seek the support of a therapist, their church, and other groups supportive of their experience.

The Kanji (Chinese pictographic writing, see below) symbol for "crisis" equates to "danger" and "opportunity."

In order to see the opportunities in something as potentially tragic as a divorce, you need a level head. While friends and family may love you, a therapist will be more objective. You need objectivity to stay out of the power struggles that the controlling person can create in a high-conflict divorce.

If at all possible, work with a mediator to craft a win-win solution to your divorce. Be willing to compromise and to walk away with a "half-fair" deal. In the long run, walking away from your money and possessions may be worth it to avoid the acrimony. Remember, it is only your perception that you are getting an unfair deal. With the dollars you save on legal fees, you can free up your life to explore a new and healthier way of living.

On the other hand, if you are up against a party who refuses to negotiate honorably, you need to use another strategy. The most important thing to consider is that your desire to be reasonable and fair may be exactly what does you in. When you seek a win-win solution, but the other party is seeking a win-lose solution, the other party is in the driver's seat, at least in our current divorce court environment.

So here is the simple answer if you do not wish to stoop to the underhanded. Do your best to secure a fair, mediated agreement. If you cannot swing a mediated agreement with the controlling party, and in very short order, don't hesitate and hope that he or she will somehow have a change of heart. You need to act swiftly before you are inundated by the divorce wars that can ensue. Give your partner what he or she wants (in terms of ego gratification such as something concrete like money or the house) and count your blessings that he or she allowed you to get away unscathed.

Never, ever, go to court with a controlling partner who wants nothing more than to trash and burn you, especially if he or she has means (i.e., money or power). And never, ever, go to court with a controlling partner if you have children to protect. The court system is designed to determine a winner and a loser – not to resolve conflict amicably and not necessarily to protect the innocent. If you are really a win-win type of person, you are no match for a system that does not hold the attacker responsible, but instead requires you to defend yourself against the constant attacks of the controlling person. You just can't keep up.

It is not easy to take the high road in these kinds of situations. Even at the cost of losing material goods or enduring a little neighborhood gossip (such as Edwin's accusations that Justine was "crazy"), trust that taking the high road means that you and your children will be able to sleep soundly at night. The gift to yourself and your family is to walk away from these divorce wars with your integrity and compassion intact.

One Woman's Solution to Divorce

Meet Isabel.

Although Isabel was stressed, she had a calmness about her. She is one of those level-headed women who know that overreacting will only make things worse. When she finally understood that the problems in her marriage were connected to her husband's AS, she was willing to work in couple's therapy to find a new way to relate. Unfortunately, after two years of therapy, things were no better. Her husband was angry and adamant that he did not meet the criteria for AS. A powerful, controlling and proud professional, he would not compromise. This left Isabel with no choice but to consider divorce.

Isabel took the high road. She let her husband know that she wanted a separation, but she did not file for divorce right away. She was willing to give her husband time to adjust to the idea of separation. She encouraged the children to visit with their daddy whenever they wanted to. She allowed him to take any furnishings from their home so he could create a familiar surrounding for him and the children in his apartment. She also allowed plentiful child visits with her husband's extended family, so that everyone knew that family traditions would be kept intact. In other words, she played to the need of her AS husband for control, structure and plenty of time to get used to the idea.

A year after her husband moved from the family home, Isabel asked for a legal separation. She explained to her husband that living separately was expensive and that it would be easier to handle their respective finances if they were legally separated. They even developed a legal parenting plan, although she was more than willing to keep everything very liberal.

Isabel took little steps, which is more acceptable to a person with Asperger's. Because it is so difficult for the Aspie to grasp the mindset of the other person, you must move slowly and logically to gain trust. The legal separation was a logical next step to living apart for a year. Although it took months to craft the separation document, Isabel laid the groundwork for acceptance of the divorce with her slow but sure progression toward her goal.

A year into the legal separation, Isabel approached her husband with the idea of selling the family home. Finances were tight. Even if they reconciled, selling the home made sense so that they could pay off the bills. Since Isabel had gradually been introducing her Asperger mate to the idea of divorce, without yet using the "D" word, he was more able to cooperate with this idea. When the house sold, Isabel gave her ex-husband his share of the equity. She bought a smaller home for herself and the children. About six months later, Isabel convinced her husband that it was more practical for him to use his share of the equity to put a down payment on a condo, rather than continue to rent.

When her ex-husband went so far as to buy a condo, Isabel knew that he would accept a divorce. In fact, when I asked him one day how things were going in his marriage, he acknowledged that he and Isabel were getting a divorce – and this was before she suggested it to him. He was on board with the idea because Isabel had helped him make the transition slowly, very slowly, years after their separation.

When Isabel finally got the divorce, she and her husband had been separated for five years. The children had adjusted to the changes. Her husband had a new home to live in, with furniture that he had once shared with his wife. (Remember it is important for those with AS to keep things the same as what they have lived with for years.) He had his finances in order and a regular routine with the children. Even though he was sad about the divorce, it was not a new idea by now, and it all seemed natural.

This is not to say that everything always went smoothly for Isabel. There were times when she sat in my office fuming with frustration or in tears over yet another heartbreak. Isabel's husband could be very stubborn and thoughtless, even with all of the conciliations she made. One day she was furious when she found out that he had asked the children to consider living with him full time because he was so lonesome. He had no idea how frightened it made the children to be placed in the middle of their parents. But Isabel got past these things and slowly but surely moved her husband toward divorce and freedom for herself, while keeping her family life stable. She sacrificed a lot of personal time and many resources to accomplish this, but it could have been a total disaster if she had moved too quickly, thus giving her husband the impression that he needed to fight her on everything.

Five years after Isabel decided to get a divorce, she was divorced, financially stable – and only then did she consider dating. This is an important reminder. No one wants to be dumped for another lover. No one is ready for another mate when in the middle of a heated divorce. Children cannot make that type of transition without lots of time to adjust. As much as you want to find happiness in a new relationship, no matter how many offers you may get, hold off until the healing is further along. Plus it is important to consider that waiting is much better than quickly choosing someone who is willing to choose you when you are still emotionally unsteady.

Lessons Learned

1. High-conflict divorce is all too common in marriages where at least one member has Asperger Syndrome, primarily because of the empathy problem.
2. If you are engaging in counterproductive behaviors in order to survive in your marriage, it is time to stop and seek professional guidance. Don't break the rules because you are unhappy.
3. If you are lucky enough to resolve your marital problems with your Asperger mate, count your blessings. But if you must get a divorce, get professional guidance on how to move forward. You are not on a level playing field. If you do not want to lose your freedom or your children, take very seriously every threat of retaliation.
4. Always take the high road in divorce. Do not move quickly, unless you are in physical danger. Plan carefully to move your partner toward acceptance of the divorce.
5. In the long run, taking your time with an Asperger mate allows him or her the comfort of the transition needed to better accept your decisions.

CHAPTER THIRTEEN

Practical Tips and Psychotherapy That Works

While this book is about understanding the nature of the Asperger-neurotypical (AS-NT) relationship, such understanding is only the first step toward problem solving and healing. Information helps build insights, but putting those insights into practice is easier said than done. I don't want to leave you an intellectual expert on Asperger Syndrome with nowhere to go to make your life and your relationship work better.

At the end of each chapter I have given you tips to follow that should help start the change process. In this chapter I move beyond tips to discuss more in-depth methods for improving the relationship. While there is a variety of treatments and interventions for autism spectrum or anxiety disorders, this book is about relationships with a significant other in your life who as Asperger Syndrome. Therefore, this chapter is dedicated to marital, family and relationship therapy. Hopefully I can show you how to use this approach to rescue your NT-Asperger relationship. When you finish this chapter you will be in better shape to find the right mental health specialist for you and your loved ones.

Tips from My Experience

If you have read this far, I hope you have gleaned a number of tips on how to resolve problems between NTs and Aspies, especially within the context of a marriage and family life. One of those tips has been reiterated in nearly every chapter, and that is to seek out a compassionate and competent psychotherapist to help guide you through the maze. I wish I could give you a step-by-step formula for curing all the psychological ills in your relationships, but treatment of Asperger Syndrome is still in its infancy.

What I can offer you is my personal and professional experience, bolstered by the theories and expertise of such notables as Maxine Aston, Tony Attwood and Temple Grandin, who recommend a very practical approach.[6]

All Things Connect

If you are ready to plunge into the discovery of who you are and how to interact more lovingly with your partner and with less defensiveness, you need to step out of your preconceived notions of the way it is, the way it should be – or even what is right and wrong. Just like Alice stepping through the Looking Glass, your life in an NT-Asperger relationship has turned your world upside down, inside out and backwards. Absolutely the only way to heal, to find peace and to create joy for yourself or with your partner, is to come to terms with a universal law . . . that all things connect.

For example, it is not an accident that you chose your partner, but it would be mind boggling to analyze all of the reasons you two came together. Culture, timing, intellectual interests, sense of humor, family background, historical trauma, even a one night stand that stretched into years . . . the list goes on and on. Instead of taking a lifetime to ferret out all of the reasons you came together, accept that there is meaning here. Accept that your partner came into your life to help you grow as a human and as a spirit. Accept

[6]See, for example, Aston, M. (2003). *Asperger's in Love: Couple Relationships and Family Affairs.* London, UK: Jessica Kingsley Publishers; Attwood, T. (2007). *The Complete Guide to Asperger's Syndrome.* London, UK: Jessica Kingsley Publishers; and Grandin, T., & Barron, S. (2005). *Unwritten Rules of Social Relationships.* Arlington TX: Future Horizons Inc.

that you are an intricately evolved being interacting and connecting with another intricately evolved being, who has been and still is interacting and connecting with other beings.

Even more incredible and incomprehensible is the fact that this process between people is also going on as we interact and connect with multiple interacting systems, large and small, such as our neighborhood, our church, the stock market, political campaigns, the workplace, our children's schools, our friends and extended family, and more. The only way to work with the mystery of stepping through the Looking Glass is to accept that this reality is created by us and for us (through our interacting and connecting) to help us learn the lessons of life and to bring love and joy to others.

This systems approach can also help you change what is not working. If we have created this reality for ourselves, then we can institute change also. In fact, we are doing that all of the time but not always consciously. Your frustrating and demanding NT-Asperger relationship provides you with the opportunity to wake up and take on the challenges of change in a conscious, constructive and loving way. We saw these conscious changes with Jeri, Miranda and Helen earlier, for example. Something clicked for Jeri when she confronted her cancer, stopped being a victim and reached out for others. Miranda developed compassion for Norman when she learned how much he had suffered. Helen's stubbornness about letting go of her reality led to a destructive episode, but out of this painful experience, she began to finally reassess her situation.

Throughout this book, I have taken this systems approach in describing the lives of people in relationship with an Asperger loved one. The only way to really know how Asperger Syndrome affects a marriage or partnership is to look at the context of the lives involved. And to create positive change, it is necessary to work with the context too . . . to create movement within and among the multiple connections and interactions that define each and every one of us.

A Diagnosis of the Mind

It may seem contradictory to such an open approach as systems theory, but the first place to start is with a diagnosis. So often I hear resentment about being "labeled." The value of a diagnosis is to point you in the right direction. Why reinvent the wheel? If there is a body of literature and therapeutic techniques that have already proven helpful to others in a similar situation, why not take advantage of it? The diagnosis is not the cure, only a starting point for healing.

It is also important to keep an open mind. Experienced and talented psychotherapists are well aware that as they gather new information, come to know their clients better and engage in the process of working with those multiple interacting systems within which their clients live, these therapists may see new diagnoses and help you create other options for change.

While psychologists and psychiatrists have a host of assessment instruments and tools to use in diagnosing many psychological disorders, there is no definitive lab test or psychological test that can diagnose Asperger Syndrome . . . or the relationship problems that emerge for an NT-Asperger couple. There are paper-and-pencil tests that can determine how severe someone's depression is or whether a person demonstrates the typical profile of someone with obsessive/compulsive disorder or alcoholism. We have good tests for determining the nature of a psychosis, and even if someone is faking an outcome. We have lab tests for thyroid disease and allergies. We have X-rays, CT scans and MRIs to take pictures of the inner workings of the body and the brain, but we have nothing remotely similar to take pictures of the inner workings of the mind and our emotions.

So how on earth do you make a diagnosis? The bottom line is that even very powerful neuropsychological tests and brain scans that can assess brain injury are not structured to be able to identify Asperger Syndrome yet. So the only way currently to diagnose is by a clinical interview. A clinical interview consists of far more than a one-hour chat. It involves gathering a substantial psychological and health history from the person, plus observations of the client from teachers, parents, spouse and others. Think about it, how do you diagnose the interpersonal relating abilities of someone with AS, unless you consult with their loved ones? Folks with AS can go undiagnosed for years because a kind but unknowing psychotherapist was unaware of the interpersonal world of his client.

While it is a good idea to supplement the clinical interview with interpersonal data, it is also very helpful to administer personality tests and tests of psychopathology. While these tests do not identify Asperger Syndrome, they do give the clinician information about certain mental states, such as "social isolation," "depression" or "anxiety." Not everyone with Asperger Syndrome is socially isolated or depressed, or even anxious. Not every NT in love with an Aspie has the same psychological profile either. However, there are common themes that should be considered when developing a treatment plan. And the treatment plan is what comes after the diagnosis.

Insight and Mind Blindness

Traditionally, psychotherapy has been about insight. That is, it is assumed that a person's ability to look within for meaning about her life experience helps her to find answers to her problems. Insight leads to analysis and a search for another method to live one's life, ideally an improved method.

But it is not enough to have insight. The psychotherapeutic process requires discussing your insights with your therapist, who then helps you analyze and develop alternative views and behaviors. This is known as a treatment plan.

Individuals with Asperger Syndrome have a very difficult time understanding or explaining their inner thoughts, whereas NTs are constantly assessing how their inner workings affect them in relationship to others. This is an example of what cognitive psychologists call Theory of Mind. If one person in the marriage is mind blind and the other has good social radar, clearly this not only affects the communication between them, it affects the direction in psychotherapy as well.

Theory of Mind was first introduced through the work of psychologists studying chimpanzees.[7]

Meet Charmaine and Rolf. They are a perfect example of this difference in ability to use insight to create change. On the day we discussed with Rolf the possibility that he has Asperger Syndrome, he was very interested in the diagnosis. It made sense to him in so many ways. Charmaine was excited too, and she began to anticipate more progress in therapy with this new revelation. In fact, she felt her hopeless feelings dissipate when Rolf made the following astute observation regarding the mind blindness that interferes in his relationships. He turned to me with a real sense of accomplishment and asked, "Do you suppose this is why my first wife left me?"

This little bit of insight is enough to keep an NT going for quite a while. But for Rolf, it was nothing more than an observation. He still was not connecting the dots. In fact, now that he had a diagnosis, he assumed that therapy was completed. Consequently, he was puzzled when his NT wife wanted to continue therapy to learn better ways of communicating across the NT-Aspie barrier. As far as he was concerned, he was successful in life in many ways. Now with a new bit of information about himself, his wife should be in a better position to understand and accept him for who he is. Needless to say, Charmaine became more depressed than ever.

Process vs. Content

Another way to look at Theory of Mind is that NTs are engaged in working with the process of the relationship, whereas Aspies are trying to understand the content or the facts. For example, Rolf accepted his diagnosis as a fact, whereas his wife saw it as a step in the process of growing closer together. Both responses are valuable parts of the equation, but on different planes of awareness.

In cases like these, the therapist either has a lot of translating to do

---

[7] See Premack, D. G., & Woodruff, G. (1978). Does the chimpanzee have a theory of mind? *Behavioral and Brain Sciences, 1,* 515-526. The Theory of Mind concept and mind blindness have been expanded beyond chimpanzees to people with autism through the work of Baron-Cohen, for example; see Baron-Cohen, S. (1995). *Mind Blindness: An Essay on Autism and Theory of Mind.* Cambridge, MA: MIT Press. The term "social radar" is a colloquialism that aptly describes the continuum from mind blind to highly empathic.

or needs to teach translating skills. I have suggested throughout the book that NTs need to learn the language of their Aspie loved one in order to bridge the communication barriers. In addition, the therapist must work independently with each person to bring him or her closer to the middle. If Rolf persists in his notion that all that is needed is agreement about his diagnosis, interpersonal growth is at a standstill. Charmaine seeks mutual understanding and respect regardless of the diagnosis. She will fail in this goal if she is the only one to work toward it.

Example of a Systems Approach

Remember Jeri and Emil? Jeri rather enjoys Emil's sense of humor. It is one of the things that bonded them when they first met. It is kind of dry and quirky, and sometimes catches her off guard in delightful ways. But Jeri has noticed things that are outside of her current understanding (or reality) of how relationships and humor interact. She remembers, for example, laughing uproariously at something Emil said at a party not long ago. When she stopped laughing, a party-goer commented, "How sweet of you to laugh at Emil's jokes!" as if no one else thought the joke was funny. Jeri had also noticed that Emil did not laugh much at other people's jokes, but then she assumed that he just didn't like their style as much.

One day as Emil, Jeri and I were meeting for therapy, I asked Emil about this question of humor. I was trying to connect the dots for Jeri and Emil. "Emil, I was wondering why it is that you don't laugh at others' jokes that often."

Before Emil could respond, Jeri interrupted with her characteristic NT protectiveness, "Oh, that's because there are only a few things that really make Emil laugh. He has a unique sense of humor, you know."

I tried again, in spite of Jeri's version of reality. "But Emil, I was wondering if the reason you don't laugh is that you don't understand the punch line. Could that be true?"

Emil looked at me earnestly. "Of course. I never really understand what they are laughing at."

Jeri looked at Emil in amazement. She had never considered that Emil thought this way before. Then the pieces started to fall into place for Jeri. Of course, Emil was able to laugh at his own jokes because he knew the context, but he was unable to follow the context of another's humor. Jeri laughed at Emil's jokes more than other people, because she loves Emil and understands the context of his life. She is very good at gathering meaning from this context. Emil has Asperger Syndrome, meaning that humor is important to Emil in and of itself, but not necessarily as a way to connect with others.

Fortunately, this situation helped Jeri and Emil look at the context of their relationship through new eyes. That is, the example of how each uses humor gave them a template for developing their interface protocol. Jeri realized that there is so much that she does not understand about Emil. She realized that she attributes NT meaning to Emil's behavior and that this can lead to conflicts.

Although Emil didn't get much from this exchange about humor, he brought in his own example at our next session. He described a film he had seen about two lovers that had given him an inkling about the contextual interaction between two people. The director and actors worked to create scenes to show what each character was thinking and feeling within several contexts. For example, when the male lead said something, the filmmakers explicitly showed what the female lead was thinking and feeling in response. Notably, the characters were not always on the same page. Emil was excited about his discovery. He said, "I realize now that there may be something totally different going on with Jeri than what I am feeling or thinking. I still don't know what she is feeling all of the time, but at least I know it might be different."

As a therapist, my job is to bring these levels of awareness together for this couple. As Jeri learns more about Aspie thinking, she can assume nothing in common with Emil unless she checks it out. She needs to learn to respectfully question what is going on with Emil because it does not always occur to him to point out the differences. Emil, on the other hand, needs a lot of practice asking Jeri about her feelings and thoughts. He may be aware that she thinks differently than he does, but he does not understand the relevance of asking her about herself. Gently asking for clarification on both sides can bring this couple closer together and out of defensiveness.

What About the Children?

I have often told the following story of my daughter Bianca that took place when she was about five years old. By then, having lived all of her life with her mommy as both a mother and a professional with an office in the home, Bianca had carefully observed her role model. On this day, Bianca was wearing a little Bavarian dress given to her by her Italian nanny. Around her waist she tied an apron. From the dress-up closet she found an old pair of my high-heeled shoes. She put her dolly in her toy baby carriage as she prepared to take her baby for a walk. The finishing touch was when she picked up a blue plastic carrying case for her crayons that looked remarkably like a miniature briefcase.

I turned to look in Bianca's direction when I heard the clippety-clop of my high heels falling off her feet, as Bianca walked toward the garage door. As she rolled her baby carriage across the kitchen floor, I smiled and asked, "Where are you going, Bianca?"

She looked over her shoulder and replied matter-of-factly, "I'm going to a meeting, Mommy." And then she continued rolling toward the door, modeling what she had seen me do many times when I would bundle up the children and take them with me on an errand – and yes, even to a professional meeting.

Children practice being adults from the day they are born, and it is our job as parents to help them grow into full-time people. But NT children and Aspie children role model differently. In the case of Bianca's play, can you tell whether she is internalizing the acts and gaining insight into her role as a girl, a woman, a mother and a professional? Or is she merely copying something she has observed and that she will incorporate into a body of rules that she will follow for the rest of her life regardless of its insight value?

The NT child will notice her mother's smile and accept the social approval of her behavior. She will add to her repertoire the skill of walking her child in the stroller on the way to a meeting, but more important to her is the loving interaction associated with the explicit skill. The love is what guides her in her development as a woman, a mother and a professional.

The Asperger child needs a different type of reinforcement to develop the explicit skill of carrying for her baby. Obviously, for healthy self-esteem, a mother's love is just as important to the Asperger child, but it is not necessarily causally related to learning the role of a woman, mother or professional. In the example above, I would need to explicitly state to Bianca that I am pleased that she is taking good care of her baby. I would have to verbally reinforce the behavior with a logical message such as, "Thank you for taking such good care of your baby and taking her to the meeting with you. This is what good mothers do. Plus it makes the baby feel loved just like I love you. That's important, isn't it Bianca?"

More than likely, an NT-Aspie marriage has produced at least one Aspie child. As we saw with Helen and Grant, their daughter has Asperger Syndrome and their son is neurotypical. Parenting these two children is as complex as it gets. One requires lots of love and coaching. The other requires lots of love . . . and long talks. When an NT-Aspie couple with children is struggling in their marriage, it is wise to consider therapy that includes the children, too.

Often I find that NT parents want to protect their NT child from the burden of building that interface protocol with Asperger family members. But the reality is that for your children, all of them, this is the family they have, and they need to get to know the system better. Just as you want to break through the communication and relating barriers so that you can connect with your loved ones, your child wants this success, too. It is no help to raise your child without the necessary skills to interact with their Aspie loved ones. And it may just be that your NT child grows immeasurably because of these lessons in life. A true measure of our life is not what we inherit but what we make of our inheritance.

Sensory Awareness, Emotional Regulation and Teachable Moments

Sensory-motor awareness and training is a huge asset to treatment and intervention for individuals with Asperger Syndrome. I haven't touched on this much, because I have been addressing the psychological skills of interpersonal connecting. However, individuals on the autism spectrum have to live with a variety of sensory issues and emotional regulation problems that can interfere with relating. They often have allergies to foods and perfumes. Flickering fluorescent lights and the ticking of a clock can be so unnerving that they shut down completely. Many with Asperger Syndrome cannot stand the feel of a stocking seam rubbing across their toes. They will forego wearing new clothes because of the scratchy labels in the collar or the smell of the chemicals in the fabric. And personal hygiene can be ignored because of over-reactivity to soaps and the pulsations of the shower. Hygiene problems can be so extreme that the Aspie is shunned because of her body odor or lack of grooming.

In order to balance the work being done in the psychologist's office with the practicality of everyday living in a multi-sensory world, I often suggest to Aspies and their family members to engage in a variety of sensory-motor techniques to help increase the Aspie's tolerance to certain stimuli and so that they can respond more appropriately to the social world.

You can seek the help of an occupational therapist who is trained in sensory integration therapy as developed by A. Ayers.[8] Also naturopaths, chiropractors, pediatric neurologists and many other health care providers offer various treatments to soften the intensity of sensory-motor problems common to those with Asperger Syndrome. Beware of the claims of success of many of these approaches, however. The research base is still limited, or nonexistent.

Along with sensory-motor integration, simple emotional regulation techniques may be used during a "teachable moment" to enhance the sensory awareness and integration of the sensory system of your Aspie loved one.

For example, Helen learned to minimize the inevitable startle response that occurred when she walked up behind Grant as he was concentrating in front of the computer. This was not just a simple startle response, but an outburst of rage resulting from Grant's inability to regulate his emotions and integrate his senses. If Helen

[8] *Sensory Integration and Learning Disabilities.* (1972). Los Angeles: Western Psychological Services.

came into the room unannounced, Grant would spin around in his chair and scream at her that she was interrupting him.

Helen was so shocked that she started to totally avoid Grant when he was working. However, when she learned that Grant, like Jasmine, has Asperger Syndrome and that both were prone to sensory overload, she developed a strategy to ease them into the fact that she was coming into the room. Helen learned to quietly announce Grant's name as she approached the room, such as "Hey Grant, I am coming to your office." Then, as she crossed the threshold, she would say again, "Hi Grant, just checking in with you." Next, a bit closer to him, she might say, "Grant, honey, dinner is nearly ready." Finally, if he had still not acknowledged her presence, Helen would stand quietly within his visual field and say, "Grant, would you like to join us for dinner?" If Grant paid attention at this point and seemed agreeable to her presence, Helen would reach over and gently touch his hand or his shoulder to reinforce the positive interaction.

This technique allowed Grant to slowly make the transition from the computer screen to his wife. Over many months of using this respectful approach, Grant began to recognize the signals that Helen was approaching long before she needed to verbally repeat herself multiple times. Not only did he recognize her presence but he acknowledged her too. That is a connection that Helen sorely needed.

Mandy developed a similar method to open up communication with Norman. Mandy found it infuriating that Norman would close his eyes and shut down completely in the middle of a conversation with her. She viewed the behavior as rude until she discovered Norman's diagnosis.

Now she realizes that Norman is overwhelmed at times by the visual field, particularly Mandy's face when it is obvious she is angry with him. He handles the problem by closing his eyes. When Mandy gets this signal, she stops talking immediately and gives Norman some breathing room. Then she asks, "Would you like to take a little break, Norman?" Even if he is too overwhelmed to talk, Mandy accepts the silence as affirmation. She leans forward and says "O.K., let's take a break. I'll be back in a moment." Sometimes this is all Norman needs to get himself back on track. Eventually, with this respectful approach Norman started to advocate for himself and ask for breaks if he needed them rather than leaving it up to Mandy to guide him.

Helen averted a major meltdown one day with Jasmine by using yet another approach in a teachable moment. She taught Jasmine a method for managing her emotions, and she helped Jason learn to have more tolerance for his sister.

Helen had returned from the grocery store and asked the twins to help put things away. Jasmine was particularly interested in rummaging through the groceries for a special food that she likes. When she couldn't find it, she looked very annoyed.

"Where's my snack?" Jasmine demanded with quite a bit of irritation in her voice.

Helen questioned Jasmine cautiously and with a low tone of voice so as not to increase Jasmine's anxiety. "What are you talking about, Jasmine? I got everything on the list. I didn't know you wanted some special snack. There are lots of things here to eat. Let's put the groceries away. Then we can sit down and have a snack."

Increasing her anger and distress, Jasmine said, "But I was waiting for this snack. I was counting on it. You don't understand how important it is to me. Didn't you listen to me when I told you what I wanted when you left for the store?"

As much as Helen wanted to confront her daughter's rudeness directly, she knew that Jasmine would explode if she did. She also realized that Jasmine's emotional regulation skills were no match for her distress at the moment. So she stepped in to guide her daughter to an alternative in this intense, but teachable moment. "Honey, I am so sorry that I missed the snack you wanted. It's too late now, but I can get it next time. Right now though, I know that you feel very upset. Do you think it would help to go to your room and listen to some music or draw for a while? Take a little break and see if you can feel better."

Jasmine was not entirely convinced, but seemed to soften. "I don't know if that will help. When I feel like this I can't think straight."

Her mother felt a wave of relief as she realized that the tantrum had been avoided. "Well, go see if that will work for you. If it doesn't work, you and I can talk again and find another option. When you feel better, come and find me and Jason. Love you, honey."

Of course, Jason had a complaint.

"Sheesh, Mom! All Jasmine has to do is yell at you and you cave. Now I have to do all the work!"

"For heaven's sake, Jason. Which would you rather have . . . an all nighter with your sister or take a half hour of your precious time to help with the groceries? Besides, you need to learn to be grateful for all of your blessings. Jasmine has a lot of work to do every moment of every day just to stay balanced, happy and on track with life."

Much to Helen's surprise, Jasmine returned about ten minutes later, composed, smiling and ready to help with the rest of the groceries. Helen gave her a hug not only because she loved her but as a way of reinforcing the more mature behavior. Then she turned to Jason and gave him a knowing wink – he smiled back. This was important, as it is important to acknowledge the adjustments Jason must make in order to help Jasmine. Hopefully, Jason also learned in this teachable moment that love conquers all.

Getting the Right Kind of Help

So much of therapy with NT-Asperger couples is directed toward the Aspie or helping the NT adjust to his or her Aspie partner. But NT partners need individual therapy also, even though they are sorely tempted to put all of their attention on therapy for their partner and family. In order to heal a relationship, two healthy people need to meet each other in the middle.

Although insight-oriented approaches are very emotionally reinforcing for NTs, they are not the only method that NTs need, especially when they are recovering from symptoms reminiscent of post-traumatic stress disorder (PTSD). As you have seen throughout the book, the lack of empathy demonstrated by their Aspie loved ones leads many NTs to lose sight of their own reality and collapse into agonizing despair.

Jason expressed this intense level of distress when he slumped under the coat rack and exclaimed that he hated his sister. Helen certainly demonstrated her PTSD-like and battered wife symptoms on numerous occasions, especially with her over-reaction to Grant's abuse and under-reaction to her self-care. Monique doubted her own sanity when all she wanted from her husband was love and intimacy. Jeri had no one with whom to share her triumph over cancer, leaving her to wonder if she was worthy of love at all.

This type of mental and emotional confusion needs powerful therapy to break through the faulty reasoning that is a result of using NT logic to make sense of the Asperger world.

Therapies that are traditionally used for PTSD and similar disorders include EMDR (eye movement desensitization and reprocessing), neuro-linguistic programming (NLP) and thought field therapy (TFT). These approaches help change the "circuits" in the brain that are so easily triggered. If you can learn to stop reacting to your partner's triggers, such as the screaming, the accusations, the concrete thinking, and certain other socially inappropriate mannerisms, you can take a more positive direction for your sense of safety and well being as well as offer help to your loved ones.

Cognitive-behavioral therapy is a very valuable way to crack deep depression. With this approach, your therapist challenges your belief system so that you can let go of dysfunctional behavior that is making you depressed. For example, Carolyn was stuck with her belief that in order to get a divorce she had to be angry with her Aspie husband or convince herself that he was bad in some way.

Blame and anger left Carolyn feeling tortured. With a cognitive-behavioral approach in therapy, she substituted a new, more healthy belief that she could leave her husband because there was no reason to stay. With this new belief she could view both herself and her husband as good people who were a mismatch as mates.

Other tools that a psychologist may use include hypnosis and a variety of reframing techniques – ways to view things from a different, more positive and healthy perspective. For example, hypnosis is a great tool for helping the NT clear up confusion about events. Hypnosis quiets the mind and allows the NT to focus on one thing at a time and to see events in a different perspective. With a new perspective, an NT has the opportunity to choose a new action. This is very freeing.

Jeri used hypnosis to redirect healing energy to her cancer cells. She also used hypnosis to clear her mind before presenting new ideas to her husband and to re-center herself after particularly trying encounters with her Aspie family members. In addition to standard hypnosis, your therapist can teach you self-hypnosis techniques to use between therapy appointments to further your progress in reclaiming your life.

As for reframing, Jeri even came to view her cancer as a benefit. There is no hope in being a helpless victim. Jeri's triumph over cancer taught her to be strong unto herself, which gave her the courage and compassion to be more objective about her husband's Asperger Syndrome.

Finally, a wonderful adjunct to individual and family psychotherapy is group therapy. But it is important to seek a group of NTs who are likewise working through the dilemma of living with an Asperger partner. Hearing others' stories, much like the ones in this book, helps NTs know that they are not alone. It is an enormous relief to realize that your anger and anguish are mirrored by others with similar experiences. Often the first step for NTs toward reclaiming their lives is when they understand that they make sense to others, if not to their Asperger loved ones. These therapy groups are few and far between, but they can work wonders to get survivors focused in a new direction . . . out of despair and toward regaining their psychological health.

Bringing It All Together

First, remember that it is no accident that you are in this NT-AS relationship. You are being offered the opportunity to find meaning in your life, a type of meaning that would never have been possible without the conflicts and confrontations of this type of relating. Drop the defensiveness and see the bigger picture. Step out of the chaos and ask yourself how you can become a wiser, more loving and compassionate person.

Creating a healing environment for an NT-Asperger couple requires the meshing of multiple interacting and connecting systems. Each member of the system needs to expand his or her consciousness to include the possibility that there is more to this picture than previously realized. There is also the need for practical application of methods to modify sensory overload. Layer by layer, the couple needs to find a way to recognize their different perspectives on reality. They need to learn methods to cut through their communication differences. If the defensiveness can be reduced, the couple might be able to once again come into contact with the bond of love that brought them together in the first place.

Lessons Learned

1. While there are currently no definitive tests for diagnosing Asperger Syndrome, a qualified professional can make the diagnosis with the help of a clinical interview, interviews or reports from loved ones and others who are significant in the Aspie's life (if they are willing and available), as well as psychological tests of personality and psychopathology.
2. Theory of Mind integrated with a systems approach to therapy is encouraged for all family members in a household where one or more members have Asperger Syndrome.
3. Defensiveness is reduced when you realize that the picture is broader than you realized. Search for the meaning that emerges from understanding that you and your loved one are products of multiple interacting and connecting systems.
4. Children, no differently than adults, need tools and understanding to work with the life they have inherited.
5. Sensory-motor treatments and emotional regulation techniques help those with Asperger Syndrome clear their space so that they can be more available to their loved ones.
6. If the problem has deteriorated to the point that the NT partner is suffering with PTSD-type symptoms, more intensive individual therapy is required such as eye movement desensitization and reprocessing, neuro-linguistic programming, hypnosis and cognitive-behavioral therapy.

CHAPTER FOURTEEN

Time to Rewrite Your Story

You have followed the lives of many people in this book, experiencing their confusion, tragedy and personal evolution. You have come to see that you are not alone, that others share your story. You have learned some methods for tackling these problems and rebuilding your relationship with an Aspie loved one. By this point in the journey, I hope you will know how to take back your life and rewrite your story in a healthier way, using the help of supportive friends, a good psychotherapist and the suggestions in this book. Now that you are at the end of the book, let this chapter be a jump-start for your recovery.

- What is the sliver in your mind?
- What is it that you need to know about yourself that will set you free?
- How will you start the journey of recovery for yourself and your AS loved ones?

It Starts with a Prayer

I hope you are not disappointed that Helen's story did not end differently – perhaps with a typical "happily ever after" theme. We all have moments of joy, and occasional bliss, but a lot of life is just plain hard work, and it can be treacherous. Helen has hard work ahead of her, as do all of us. But with awareness and taking full responsibility for your own life, you stand a better chance of creating more joy and serenity.

Remember the Serenity Prayer. It really should be your mantra on a daily basis.

God grant me the serenity
To accept the things I cannot change;
Courage to change the things I can;
And the wisdom to know the difference.

This simple little prayer has guided many co-dependents to recovery. It has helped many overly responsible, kind multitaskers break free from taking on the weight of the world. And it will help you too as you build your "interface protocol," or that system of translating between "operating systems" so aptly described in the introduction to this book by the Aspie engineer who wanted to rebuild his marriage to an NT partner.

How ironic that the door to serenity can open by integrating a computer term and a spiritually inspired mantra. The process of serenity grows when we learn to cherish the humanity in each of us, NT and Aspie alike.

Letting Go of Your Dysfunctional Past

It took me a while to gain that serenity. The prayer helped, and it still hangs on the wall above my computer screen . . . and in my kitchen . . . and in my bedroom. But there was a lot more work I had to do to free myself from my dysfunctional thinking and acting.

When you grow up with an Asperger parent, it can be like that. I kept looking into my mother's face for a reflection of who I am, but all I saw was my mother. I knew I wasn't my mother, but she rarely reinforced who I am. Children need help with this part of growing up. But since I didn't get it from her, I found other ways to take care of myself and build my self-esteem. Like so many of you, I developed co-dependent ways and demonstrated symptoms similar to those of post-traumatic stress disorder (PTSD), so I needed to learn different ways.

Even so, as I was gaining an understanding of my mother's part in my life and how her untreated Asperger Syndrome clouded so much of our relationship, I still stubbornly clung to my co-dependency. After all, it made me feel strong and safe. I worried about my mother, even in death. I worried that she was still suffering or had some penance to pay for the way she had treated me. I wanted her to be forgiven. And I wanted her to forgive me. I felt bad that I hadn't been there for her when she needed someone to know what was in her heart and mind. She had been so lonely all of her life, and even as she was dying I could not understand her.

I had an opportunity to check this worry out one night on a red-eye flight back from California to my home in Washington.

There were few passengers, so it was easy for me to find several rows of empty seats at the back of the plane, behind the wings where it is noisy . . . the kind of noise that drowns out everything. I found a spot, leaned back in the chair and pulled a blanket over me. But instead of going to sleep, I decided to meditate on Mom. I closed my eyes and quietly chanted a soothing mantra for a few moments, while I asked the universe if my Mom was O.K.

Soon I was startled by the pleasant fragrance of roses. Thinking that someone had come to sit in my row, and being a bit embarrassed to have the person find me chanting, I opened my eyes and sat upright. But there was no one there. Perhaps somebody had just passed by on the way to the restroom, I thought. I looked behind me at the lavatories but couldn't see well in the darkened space, so I settled back into my meditation again.

As soon as I closed my eyes and initiated my request a second time, I smelled the roses again, immediately. Again I opened my eyes, thinking whoever was in the lavatory must have passed by again. But again there was nobody there. No one.

For a third time, I went back into meditation. And for a third time I made the same request of the universe. Is Mom O.K.? Is she happy? Is she safe? Again, the roses. But this time I accepted the gift. I didn't resist. I didn't make excuses. I didn't control the outcome. I let the fragrance surround me with love and I stayed with it throughout the flight home.

It is hard to let go of old beliefs, especially when they are forged in childhood. Being the quintessential survivor, a stubborn co-dependent and a take-charge person, all of which I learned at the tutelage of my Aspie mother, I needed three repeat messages before I realized that the universe had sent me my answer. Many believe that the fragrance of roses is the sign of a spiritual master, a loving presence come to bring you comfort. After this experience, I no longer doubted that my mother was O.K. or that she was forgiven or that I was forgiven, or for that matter, that all those childhood experiences are even relevant any more. I let go of Mom and she let go of me in that moment. That is serenity.

Live with Contradictions

After about a year in therapy, Miranda told me privately, "I'm falling in love with Norman all over again . . . but he's still so cold." She smiled sweetly, not the sarcastic smile of our first few therapy sessions, but a loving, knowing kind of smile, as if she had finally accepted her husband for who he is.

"I know. It is odd, isn't it? Do you think you have come to know deep down inside that you are loved, even if Norman is not good at showing you his love? Do you think that you know you are loved, even if the love is not coming from Norman?"

"Yes, I think that's what I mean. I know that I love him and I know that I am loved too, but I have to remind myself of that a lot.

My friends and the kids help, too. And what I mean by 'cold' is that he doesn't say the things I would like to hear or do the things that would mean so much to me. Nonetheless Norman is a good man and takes care of us. That is his way of loving me. I know now that he is holding nothing back. When I thought he was withholding love, I felt awful. Now I know he is just 'cold.'" Miranda laughed a little when she used the word "cold" because she means that in such a different way now than she did when she first came to therapy.

These are the kinds of contradictions you learn to live with when you are an NT married to an Aspie or have an Aspie loved one. You love them even if they are cold. You love them even if they are blunt and appear abusive. You love them when they have "meltdowns" because you now understand how tense and busy their brains are. You love them because they need your love and comfort and understanding. They don't get that from too many people.

And when you let go of trying to change them, a miracle happens. They don't change, but you do. When you finally learn to "Accept the things I cannot change," you develop wisdom. Did you realize that at least half of those fights, those "meltdowns," those terrorizing moments with your Aspie loved one, were caused by your desire to "help"? When you accept that it is not up to you to change them, that you are not failing to "reach" them or that you are not losing because there is "no connection," . . . well things just work better.

This is detachment. This is waking up to reality. And it is a relief.

Loosen the Sliver

The *sliver in the mind* metaphor that has been used throughout the book can represent several levels of waking up. One level is the realization that came to Helen, Jeri and Mandy – that while everything looked perfectly normal on the outside for them and their husbands, there was a lack of connection between them. You aren't really connecting or loving another if you don't speak their language. Learning to speak the language of Asperger's in order to connect with your Aspie loved one is a major challenge. While this is an unpopular opinion among some, I still believe it is far easier for NTs, who have the greater empathy skills, to learn the language of their Asperger's loved one than it is for those with Asperger's to speak the language of their NT loved ones. However, what those with Asperger's can do is to acknowledge this challenge. That little bit of understanding goes a long way with an NT.

Another level of waking up is realizing that co-dependency and anxiety, shell shock and survivor stress are only ways of coping, not ways of embracing life. Don't blame yourself for these choices. It is understandable that you made them, given the confusion and desperation you felt living with AS. But you have other tools now. As long as you stubbornly cling to these crippling coping mechanisms, you will feel miserable and make those around you miserable, too.

A third level of waking up is to know that you are alone in your discoveries – and yet you are not alone. There will be few who truly know what it is like to live an NT-Asperger life. You can explain, explain and explain, but you are likely to hear back such comments as, "But aren't all husbands like that?" Rather than feeling sorry for yourself that you happen to have this particular burden, take it on and be responsible for a successful outcome. It could take years, but who better to do your life than you. After all, you are the only person you will live your whole life with. Do it well.

There are many other levels, too. The sliver is a wonderful metaphor. Keep working it until you free every sliver that is bothering you. For example, you may discover that you have some Asperger traits yourself. Or you may revel in the NT-like empathy that comes from your Asperger's loved one when he is able to relax around you, no longer worried about disappointing you. Other possibilities include waking up to talents and dreams that have long been on hold in your life because you have been preoccupied with what is "wrong." Start thinking about what is "right" and let the problems cure themselves for a change. Don't hold back any longer. Go live your life as fully as you can instead of waiting for anyone to join you.

Finally, another level to consider is whether you have the stamina to stay in a relationship with an Aspie if you have a choice. These relationships can be very fatiguing, demoralizing or worse. Yes, there are ways to make it work, but for some the price is too great. The example below highlights this. It certainly made me consider the stresses that this life has upon the NT children in the family.

One day my daughter was hanging out in my office doing her homework at my secretary's desk. One of my clients came in and mistook her for my secretary and chatted with her a while about business. My daughter, about sixteen at the time, was polite but puzzled that the client was treating her like my office manager instead of my daughter, especially since she had seen this man many times before. But apparently he didn't recognize her, or wasn't sure how to converse with her on subjects more relevant to a teen.

Later she came to me and asked if this man has Asperger Syndrome. I told her that I could not reveal confidential information, but I was curious about what made her think so and asked her.

She gave me one of those patronizing teenage looks and said, "You know, Mom, I kind of know when someone has Asperger's."

"Oh, and how do you know that?" I asked with surprise.

"Well, I know they have Asperger's," she said, "because when you talk with them, it makes you want to shoot ***your*** *brains out."*

Even in this short little encounter, my daughter felt the strain of the lack of connection with this man, the unfathomable disability of some Aspies who can't remember a face, and the social pressure to continue a conversation with someone when it makes no sense. Just think of how this strain grows day after day, month after month, year after year and how troubling it is to take care of yourself in these relationships, let alone help your children too.

So it is very important for you to consider whether you are willing or even able to manage the strain or if all would be better off if you left the marriage. For example, if your partner refuses to go to therapy with you, you may have no choice but to leave. As in any relationship, both people create the situation they live in. If only one of you is taking responsibility for your growth, you will soon outstrip your partner. This is the kind of imbalance we saw when Helen exploded into violence because of Grant's abuse. Far better to call the whole thing off than to let your life deteriorate this way. A lot more can be said about this option, but I suggest you discuss this with a good psychologist so that you are prepared for the tumult a divorce can cause.

Allowing and Compassion

Everything Is Just So

If you choose to stay, wake up and take responsibility and embrace one of life's toughest adventures, you need to develop the skills of *allowing* and *compassion* in order to bridge the worlds of Asperger's and NTs. A young woman with Asperger's has taught me these two principles, although she doesn't know it.

When this young woman was about fourteen, she drew two pictures that convey more to me about her life with Asperger Syndrome than dozens of books ever could. Through her art and music, she shares the deepest parts of herself. Once she said to her mother, "I wish others could just read my mind," so that she would not have to struggle with conversation.

But she shouldn't worry about that. The window to her mind is clearly seen in her art. These two drawings have helped me create allowing and compassion in my life, too. And I am so grateful that her mother shared these drawings and personal memories with me for my book.

On the cover of this book is a drawing of a young girl, barefoot and pole vaulting off the edge of a cliff – into nothingness. She never told her mother what she intended by this drawing, but art is like that. The artist leaves the message to the viewer. To me, this pencil drawing represents both Aspies and NTs. In our troubling relationships with loved ones, it feels as if we are pole vaulting into nothingness – that there is no place to land or connect to and get some peace from the turmoil.

But another way to look at this drawing is that it represents a beginning of an adventure. Going over the edge means it's time to leave the world as you have assumed it to be. Jump off the cliff and expect that there is a place to land. I hope that after reading this book, you can see that there is some firm ground to land on, even though you may have to make some remarkable changes in your perception of reality and the TRUTH.

This drawing also represents the skill of *allowing* or just going with what life gives you. In therapy, this young woman's mom shared these realizations with me. She didn't expect to adopt a child with Asperger Syndrome. She didn't expect to have her notions of parenting turned upside down. She didn't expect her child to be tormented by anxieties. She didn't expect that all of her organized and reasoned life would not be enough to reach her cherished child. But by coming to accept what *is* in her life, she is in a much better position to see all of the resources and love that is available to her and her daughter. And by accepting what *is*, she is much better able to stop sorting for the right answers.

One day when this clever little girl was about five, she told her mother, "You know Mommy, we don't look alike." Since she is adopted, it was not surprising that some day she would put this together, even though her mother had never told her otherwise. Both of her parents have always been open about her adoption and even celebrate her adoption day. But rather than putting words into her mouth and running with assumptions about what was in her mind, her mother smartly decided to ask her what she meant by that comment. Very seriously and in a matter-of-fact Asperger way, the child observed, "Well, Mommy, you have short hair and mine is long." Nothing more than that. Nothing deep. No worry about her birth parents. Just an observation. How droll.

This is what allowing is about. Have the courage to accept things as they are and make no more meaning out of them than that. Everything really is just so.

Compassion Is Believing in the Other Person

The second picture I have saved for this last chapter of the book. It is a self-portrait drawn by this young woman about the same time as she drew the cliff picture. According to her mother, the child again made no comment on the meaning behind the drawing. It was an assignment for school. All of the children were asked to draw a self-portrait.

Her mother was so proud of her daughter's talent that she copied the drawing and taped it to the bookcase in her office. In fact, she was so proud of the drawing that she made a copy for me, and I also hung it on my office bulletin board. She thought it a marvelously detailed abstract drawing, even if a bit disturbing, but she long ago had learned to accept the dark side of her Aspie daughter.

However, the mother did not truly see the whole picture when she first saw it. Neither did I. It looked like a collage of animals, real and mythical. Her daughter loves to draw animals, so her mother assumed the self-portrait was a gathering of her daughter's favorite animal drawings, even the fanged ones, until one day when her daughter came into my office after a session with her mother, noticed the drawing displayed on my bulletin board and matter-of-factly said, "How do you like the bats flying out of my nose?"

I was so startled by her comment that my eyes darted to the picture. Then I lost my breath, and my heart jumped into my throat. Her mother looked terrified. I now saw that this self-portrait was a profile of her daughter and that there were indeed bats flying out of her nose and snakes poised above her lips. Her left hand is outstretched in the picture with the four fingers portrayed as animals, but the (opposable) thumb is a cloaked woman, a small statement to her humanity. At the top of her head wolves are howling. Into her ear a large bird is screeching. The body and head are filled with all sorts of creatures, fish, birds, horses, dinosaurs, insects and so on. And crouched in the middle of the drawing with her legs drawn up tightly to her chest, hiding behind all of these wild animals, . . . is a frightened little girl.

I was stunned into silence when I recognized this message. Is this what is meant by a "noisy" brain, the commonly used euphemism for those with Asperger Syndrome? "Noisy" is hardly the word I would use to describe this drawing. "Frightening" is more like it. "Devastating." "Crushing." I now understand what this young woman deals with on a daily basis. No wonder it is hard for her to track what is going on with others. No wonder she craves solitude. No wonder she has little sympathy for the small problems of others. No wonder she has meltdowns when the pressures of her mind become too much. No wonder she keeps herself busy with art and the computer and music all of her waking hours and sometimes even waking up from her sleep to do more. No wonder she feels alone and is not sure of her parents' love for her. If I just post her drawing on the bulletin board and do not see the message, she must think I am the "cold" one.

Compassion requires that you understand and offer comfort to those who need it from you, but it is important not to take over for them. Compassion means conveying your belief in their competency to handle a tough situation. That is an important way of being there for another person. I can understand how a mother would desperately want to free her daughter from the craziness I saw in this girl's drawing. But that is co-dependency at its worst. Instead, her mother can be compassionate by believing in her. She can admire her daughter's courage to take on this life of Asperger Syndrome. She can be amazed by her ability to find a way to communicate through her art. Her mother can encourage her daughter to keep teaching us all to learn more about ourselves through her unique gift. Most important, mothers can love their children until the day they die and like my mother send them the scent of roses to know that we are both O.K.

In order to keep balance in your life with an Asperger's loved one, think about this young woman's self-portrait or Norman's story of childhood bullying. Talk to your family members and find out their stories of growing up with AS. This may help you hang in there when they do the "darnedest things." If you take a deep breath before you get annoyed or hurt or reach out to rescue, and if you ask yourself, "What is s/he trying to tell me by this action?" you might just get the answer. It is probably as obvious as these two incredible drawings.

Thank You

Thank you for reading this far. You are courageous and determined. Otherwise you would not have been willing to pick up this book and look for answers. And you would not have read this far only to learn that the answers are within you. You have lived with crushing, oppressive relationships. You have felt that you were going over the edge. You have felt helpless to do anything for your loved ones. At times, you even came to despise some of these family members for making the relationships so hard. Now I hope you can leave those self-defeating behaviors behind and take charge of the wonderful life you were born to live. It's time to rewrite your story.

Remember that you are not alone. Let me know how it goes. I would love to hear from you.

Kathy J. Marshack, Ph.D.
info@kmarshack.com
www.kmarshack.com

Advance Praise

Below is a sample of what others have said after reading Chapter One online. I have received literally hundreds of these kinds of emails from all over the world. I hope you gain this kind of excitement as you go through this book and begin to believe that you can come alive again.

OMG, Kathy!
Just read your chapter, it is INCREDIBLE!!!
Your words flowed, You had me in tears!!!!!
Please get this out there!!! I will help you any way I can.
This is exactly what I had always envisioned in my head but could never put into action.
Keep up the great work and GET THIS OUT THERE!!!! WE NEED TO BE HEARD!!!
I'm too emotional right now, can't wait to meet you . . .
Hugs, L . . .

Dear Dr. Marshack,
Ooh, I am desperately seeking a book such as this. Have your editors rush the publishing please. And thank you for making the first chapter available online. It was like a wisp of fresh air after years of helpless gasping for oxygen. I know I'm not the only one trapped like this who needs a lifeline and a roadmap from someone who understands and believes. (Could there truly be hope for My Life in AS-Marriage Prison?)
S . . .
[Quebec, Canada]

I am interested in the book, "Life with a Partner or Spouse with Asperger Syndrome: Going over the Edge?" I am an NT woman and was married to an AS man. Five years ago, we went through a hellish divorce. It was a horrific experience after 14 years of a "walking on eggshells" marriage. I am now a single parent raising both our sons who have AS. I could not believe how closely your FAQs described my experiences.
C . . .

Dear Dr. Marshack,
I am divorced from my ex husband A . . . for three years now who was diagnosed with Asperger Syndrome shortly before we separated. Even though we are divorced it feels like he still continues to control mine and my . . . daughter's happiness. We live in Dubai. Please help. N . . .
[Dubai]

Hello,
My name is L . . . and two weeks ago my husband of three years was diagnosed with AS. There is a mountain of information about dealing with this with children, but very little about dealing with this in marriage with an adult. I would appreciate any info you can give me about where I can purchase this book.
Thank you L . . .

Yes, please let me know when your book is available. I definitely need to order it. It will need to be posted to Australia. When do you think it will be ready?
Cheers, A . . .
[Australia]

Please could you let me have details of your book, "Life with a Partner or Spouse with Asperger Syndrome: Going over the Edge?" I have searched far and wide for something to help me deal with the pain, depression and ill health caused by twenty-four years with a husband who I am convinced has undiagnosed high-functioning Asperger's. We are now going through a very messy divorce and no one understands what I have had to deal with all these years. I can relate to Helen's story so well – I have my own similar experiences of my husband sleeping through severe illness – such as on a camping holiday when I was coughing so badly I vomited in our bed and he slept on. The worse incident, however, happened with my elderly parents when he walked past them to go to the bathroom in the night and ignored the fact that my terminally ill father was having a fatal heart attack. He came back to bed and didn't tell me!
G . . .
[UK]

Thank you. Thank you for this site. I'm crying with sadness, loneliness, and relief after reading your information on Aspies. My husband of eighteen years was diagnosed with social anxiety disorder a few years when we went to marriage counseling. I think she was close but didn't get to his Asperger's . . . her husband was transferred and she had to pack up her shop within one month. At any rate, THANK you for your information. I don't feel so helpless, so alone. I still feel sadness, but I think it's more of mourning than anything else. Mourning the loss of a marriage that will never be completely fulfilling to me. I won't divorce. Well, maybe not until the children are grown.
Thankfully, P . . .

As someone who has been in an on/off relationship, for almost two years now, with a man whom I believe strongly to have Asperger Syndrome, I would be desperate to read your book "Life with a Partner or Spouse with Asperger Syndrome: Going over the Edge?" Fingers crossed that your book soon hits the bookshops! Thanks in anticipate of hearing of its publication when it happens.
Regards, M . . .
[Scotland]

I cannot put into words how illuminating this information has been for me. I spent several fruitful hours looking at various websites, blogs, and discussion groups related to adult AS. My husband and I are both fifty-seven, lost a spouse and partner to death a few years ago, and married two and half years ago. It is just amazing how all the puzzle pieces have fallen into place to reveal a picture, not a pretty one, but a picture nonetheless. I am not crazy; I am not unlovable; I am not gullible. And he is not a mean-spirited, immature, selfish deceiver. I would like to know when your book will be available.
L . . .

Please send me a copy of your book or inform me how to order! I will be waiting eagerly!
J . . .
[Singapore]

I found your website and became interested in your book "Life with a Partner or Spouse with Asperger Syndrome: Going over the Edge?" I would be interested in buying the book, but I didn't know if you ship/ mail them outside your country, since I live in Finland, Europe? I am married to a man with Asperger Syndrome!
With best regards, K . . .
[Finland]

Dear Mrs. Marshack!
I would very much like to buy your upcoming book when it is available.
Regards,
M . . .
[Sweden]

Kathy J. Marshack, Ph.D., P.S., is a licensed psychologist with more than 25 years' experience as a marriage and family therapist and business coach. Dr. Marshack has written two previous books, a variety of articles and a family business column, and is a contributor to the nationally acclaimed *Sixty Things to Do When You Turn Sixty.* She has been profiled by national and local media, such as CNN, the Lifetime Channel, and National Public Radio.